Samuel French Acting Ed

The Revolving Cycles Truly and Steadily Roll'd

by Jonathan Payne

SAMUELFRENCH.COM   SAMUELFRENCH.CO.UK

FOR PRODUCTION ENQUIRIES

UNITED STATES AND CANADA
Info@SamuelFrench.com
1-866-598-8449

UNITED KINGDOM AND EUROPE
Plays@SamuelFrench.co.uk
020-7255-4302

Each title is subject to availability from Samuel French, depending
upon country of performance. Please be aware that THE REVOLVING
CYCLES TRULY AND STEADILY ROLL'D may not be licensed by
Samuel French in your territory. Professional and amateur producers
should contact the nearest Samuel French office or licensing partner to
verify availability.

MUSIC USE NOTE

Licensees are solely responsible for obtaining formal written permission from copyright owners to use copyrighted music in the performance of this play and are strongly cautioned to do so. If no such permission is obtained by the licensee, then the licensee must use only original music that the licensee owns and controls. Licensees are solely responsible and liable for all music clearances and shall indemnify the copyright owners of the play(s) and their licensing agent, Samuel French, against any 'causets, expenses, losses and liabilities arising from the use of music by licensees. Please contact the appropriate music licensing authority in your territory for the rights to any incidental music.

IMPORTANT BILLING AND CREDIT REQUIREMENTS

If you have obtained performance rights to this title, please refer to your licensing agreement for important billing and credit requirements.

THE REVOLVING CYCLES TRULY AND STEADILY ROLL'D was first produced by Playwrights Realm in New York, New York on September 7, 2018. The performance was directed by Awoye Timpo, with sets by Kimie Nishikawa, lights by Stacey Derosier, sound by Luqman Brown, costumes by Andrea Hood, and props by Alexander Wylie. The production stage manager was Kara Kaufman. The cast was as follows:

MAIN PLAYERS

KARMA. . . . . Kara Young

MADAM ROSE PROFÍT . . . . Lynda Gravátt

THE ENSEMBLE

THE BARBER / GOTTO / BALL PLAYER 2 . . . . Keith Randolph Smith

THE OLD TEACHER / THE POLICE OFFICER. . . . . Kenneth Tigar

FOSTER MOM / THE EX / GOTTO'S BOY 3. . . . . Deonna Bouye

YOUNG WOMAN / THE MOTHER / THE PROTÉGÉ . . . . . Toni Ann DeNoble

BALL PLAYER 1 / DANTE / GOTTO'S BOY 1 / YOUTH . . . . Donnell E. Smith

BALL PLAYER 3 / DEATH / GOTTO'S BOY 2 / THE FRIEND . . . James Udom

CHARACTERS

MAIN PLAYERS

KARMA – (17) F, black. The lone detective.

MADAM ROSE PROFÍT – (65) F, black. Proprietor of the Amigone
Funeral Home, Inc.

[handwritten: is it sexual?]

[handwritten: overseer of the street urchins]

THE ENSEMBLE

THE BARBER – (30s) M, black. Also plays **BALL PLAYER 2** and **GOTTO**

THE OLD TEACHER – (60s) M, white. Also plays **THE POLICE OFFICER**

FOSTER MOM – (20s) F, black. Also plays **THE EX** and **BOY 3**

YOUNG WOMAN – (20s) F, black. Also plays **THE MOTHER** and
THE PROTÉGÉ

BALL PLAYER 1 – (20s) M, black. Also plays **DANTE, BOY 1,** and **YOUTH**

BALL PLAYER 3 – (20s) M, black. Also plays **BOY 2, THE FRIEND,** and
DEATH

ON CASTING

Casting can vary from production to production, but I intended a cast
of 8 actors (4f, 4m) to comprise the play. There are two major players,
Karma and Profít but the rest of the characters can be divided as the
director sees fit. Ages listed for the minor characters are a point of
reference, with the intention of young playing old and old playing young.
It must be noted that the Police Officer and the Old Teacher are both
intended to be white men.

SETTING

The Oblong: An Inner City

TIME

Present Day

NOTE

A slash (/) indicates overlapping dialogue

This is not only one man, this the father of those who shall be
    fathers in their turns,
In him the start of populous states and rich republics,
Of him countless immortal lives with countless embodiments
    and enjoyments.

How do you know who shall come from the offspring of his
    offspring through the centuries?
(Who might you find you have come from yourself, if you could
    trace back through the centuries?)

                    "I Sing the Body Electric" by Walt Whitman

                    For Markeeda

PRE-SHOW

(An Inner City. A Marketplace.)

(Somewhere in the space. Dealers pitch their goods, runners stuff their stash, ladies petition their men, fiends scrounge and haggle, hustlers flash their wares, beggars charm the strapped.)

(A change happens.)

(And this sad collection.)

(Eventually.)

(With some time.)

(Huddles into a mass.) ~~reminds me of players | a greek choms~~

THE ENSEMBLE. The Oblong is an inner city, that is shaped like an inconsistent oval. It houses the forgotten, the marginalized, the poor.

People. They just people.

The Oblong doesn't know progress. It is chaos. Despite the law who calls itself order. That feeds the disease by intimidation, or prison, or homicide.

It is like an island, The Oblong, isolated by poverty. So it circulates its own economy.

By hustlin'

By drugs

By prostitution

By any means necessary.

And now that the law has removed the Old Hustlers, the Youth has filled the gap.

And they are at war with themselves.

The youth.

They draw lines in The Oblong.

Southside!

North End!

The blood that runs down these streets from skirmishes and retaliations are a rushing river.

And no end in sight.

Hence the chaos.

Hence the gunfire like unpatriotic fireworks.

Hence the dilapidated classroom.

Hence the thriving funeral home.

Hence the sirens calling through the night.

Hence the screaming mother.

Hence the hurt-sport dad.

Hence the widow orphan child.

Hence

Hence

Hence...

And so we the Ensemble

By will of the Playwright

With hope of some clarity

Present to you

A play in two acts:

THE REVOLVING CYCLES TRULY AND STEADILY ROLL'D!

ACT ONE

Prologue

*(December 13. Recent widow and inheritor of
Amigone Funeral Home,* **MADAM ROSE PROFÍT**
*cries for the community and chastises them
in the next breath.)*

*(Amigone Funeral Home. A viewing room.
A* **BARBER***, in his fifties, is in attendance.*
MADAM PROFÍT*, dressed in mourning,
addresses the audience.)*

PROFÍT. What am I wearing?

(She presents herself.)

I understand this question is obvious, but specifically...

(She presents herself again.)

Come on. Speak up. This is not to be comfortable.
There is no relaxing tonight. This is heavy stuff. Heavy.
Stuff.

Now... This isn't a hard question people – I will
rephrase it.   → Reminds me of the start
What is specific about what I am wearing?   of Hamlet

(She waits for an answer. She better get it.)

Right. Right. I am dressed in mourning. And I am
always dressed this way. You want to know why? I wear
these blacks not only for the many bodies that pass
through my doors – and there are many, many bodies –
I wear them for the youth of The Oblong. Specifically
the men – boys. All the boy bodies that flood my
viewing room, that wear down my embalming table,

that show me that I do not have the resources or the time to compensate. And I am not the only funeral home. There are three others in The Oblong, filled to the brim.

My name is Madam Rose Profít. Pro-fee! The "o" is an "o" not an "ah" and the "t" is silent. Pro-fee. I am the owner of Amigone Funeral Home, Inc., and I have called this meeting to bare witness to the misrepresentation and vilification of our black community.

Just last week, we all heard the story of young Wade Lyons, seventeen, who got in a car accident just outside of The Oblong, and crawling from the wreckage, bleeding from head to toe, limping for his life, knocked on a door to a nearby home, looking for help. And this white citizen behind the door, for whatever reason, called the police, and Wade continued to knock out of desperation, out of a need, out of sheer necessity, screaming for help, and just when he gave up, the police arrived, demanding poor Wade – bloodied, bleeding from the crown of his head – to get down on his knees. And rightfully angered by the matter he lurched forward towards the police, trying to explain what had happened. And for some odd reason he was shot four times. His right hand. His right foot. His left shoulder. His right side.

Boxed in. Vilified. My people. I call attention to this young man, and his family. And I cry for them...

> *(She tries but she does not cry. Someone, somewhere, laughs. She continues despite the outburst.)*

I cry for them. We are gathered here today to address an epidemic. And you don't even know it's an epidemic – a tragedy. YOU.

> *(She points to someone in the crowd.)*

You don't even know it, but you are to blame, you quiet stagnant mass.

THE BARBER. You can't do that –

PROFÍT. Assuming such things of our –

THE BARBER. Come on now, Mrs. Profit –

PROFÍT. Pro-fee!   ⌐————→ status — French pronunciation

THE BARBER. Pro-fee! You can't be invitin' folk here insultin'em –

PROFÍT. Curtis. I appreciate your thoughts –

THE BARBER. They are concerned citizens –

PROFÍT. Curtis. I have the floor –

THE BARBER. You lucky this many people showed up tonight any damn way –

PROFÍT. Curtis!

THE BARBER. Ain't many folk interested –

PROFÍT. SHUT! UP!

THE BARBER. Well since you asked so nicely.

PROFÍT. Concerned citizens who haven't done a damn thing about it.

THE BARBER. And what have you done?

PROFÍT. I've called this meeting.

THE BARBER. (*Aside.*) Ladies and Gentlemen, she called a meeting.

PROFÍT. I have grown tired of ignorance and apathy, Curtis. I am a product of the Civil Rights Movement. When society turned its back on us, we turned society right back around.

THE BARBER. I was there too, Madam Pro-fee. But when I was walkin' these streets in the sixties I wasn't constantly checkin' my shoulders. Different times.

PROFÍT. Different times? The people are still accountable.

THE BARBER. (*Aside.*) She is somethin'.

PROFÍT. I want to create a coalition – a network. If those that can help aren't putting us front and center, then I hope to pick up the mantle.

THE BARBER. (*Aside.*) I left my cape at the cleaners.

PROFÍT. We should own the streets, give families their backbone, pull this city out from the dark, and make it the shiny temple on the hill.

[handwritten: → another nod to historical theatre]

THE BARBER. *(Aside.)* Watch her go.

PROFÍT. Curtis. We're going to start an initiative.

THE BARBER. What's our initiative?

PROFÍT. A place where the forgotten people of The Oblong can gather to better themselves.

THE BARBER. Better themselves. You don't say.

PROFÍT. I'm sure you've heard the Mayor has issued an RFP.

THE BARBER. A what?

PROFÍT. A request for proposals, Curtis. The Mayor seeks programs to revitalize the city. I'm talking millions. And The Oblong shouldn't be last in line like it always is. We should have access to those funds. And guess what?

THE BARBER. Oh lord.

PROFÍT. I have an audience with the Mayor. A little tête-à-tête to discuss my idea, before the new year!

THE BARBER. Well good luck to you.

PROFÍT. Where do you think you're going?

THE BARBER. I ain't no hero Madam Pro-fee, and I ain't no martyr neither. I'm just a barber.

PROFÍT. Who is apathetic, like the rest of them.

THE BARBER. Oh come on, Madam Profit –

PROFÍT. Pro-fee!   *[handwritten: idea of clear status in characters]*

> *(The laughter returns, it has become irrepressible. So has* **MADAM PROFÍT**'s *anger.)*

Ex-cuse me...
Are you laughing?

> *(The laughter belongs to* **KARMA** *who appears from the crowd.)*

KARMA. Yo my lady, my lady, sorry to interrupt, but I just came to ask you somethin'.

PROFÍT. Do you find what we're talking about funny?

KARMA. Nah, you just got mad speakin' skills, my lady! You're a poet and don't even know.

(Beat.)

PROFÍT. It. Poet and you don't even know it. That's how it goes.

KARMA. How long this gonna take?

THE BARBER. What did you want to say, young lady?

PROFÍT. If you aren't here for the meeting, then you don't belong here. If it's business, you can come back tomorrow.

KARMA. Fuck. We can't talk after?

PROFÍT. Watch your language young man – lady...

THE BARBER. She just got a question –

PROFÍT. Curtis!

KARMA. Real quick. Then you can get back to it.

PROFÍT. What is it?

KARMA. This shit's kinda hard to get out.

PROFÍT. Go on with it.

KARMA. I'm just gonna ask it. You seen this kid...before?

*(**KARMA** presents a piece of paper.)*

PROFÍT. No.

THE BARBER. Don't look familiar.

KARMA. No? You ain't fuckin' with me.

PROFÍT. I am not *messing* with you.

KARMA. I know you see a lotta dead bodies, must be hard to remember everybody...

PROFÍT. I do.

KARMA. 'Cause if I have to come back in this joint –

PROFÍT. I don't recognize his name. Now can you leave? I find you irritating.

KARMA. Lady, you as stiff as the motherfuckin' bodies that come up in here. Fuck. I'm just askin' / 'bout somebody I ain't seen –

PROFÍT. GET OUT!! You dirty little hood rat!

THE BARBER. *(Aside.)* And just a minute ago she was cryin'
for these dirty little hood rats.

KARMA. Seems you a little sensitive.

PROFÍT. I'm just tired of you little corner hoodlums, / acting
up, ruining it for the worthwhile kids out there!

KARMA. Corner hoodlums?

> *(***KARMA*** laughs at this.)*

PROFÍT. Don't you know this is how they see you? How they
see us.

KARMA. They?

> *(***PROFÍT*** turns her around to the crowd.)*

PROFÍT. Them.

> *(They look out. A moment passes. ***KARMA***
> looks to ***MADAM PROFÍT***. She suddenly snatches
> ***MADAM PROFÍT****'s hat off. ***MADAM PROFÍT*** tries to
> get it back.)*

OUT! Out, I said! Before I get you locked up where you
belong!

KARMA. Alright, Corpse Lady!

> *(***KARMA*** gives her the hat back. She then pulls
> out a pad and writes something.)*

PROFÍT. What are you doing?

KARMA. Making sure I remember...

PROFÍT. You've got ten seconds.

> *(***KARMA*** starts deliberately slow. She might be
> counting to ten.)*

KARMA. Peace!

> *(Eventually she exits.)*

THE BARBER. You ain't right, Madam Pro-fee.

PROFÍT. Well are you with me or not?

THE BARBER. With you for what?

PROFÍT. My initiative. My community center. The Mayor's
coming the end of –

THE BARBER. If you don't like the neighborhood, why don't you leave? You uprooted a historical funeral home from a street it's been on for 100 years, and put yourself right smack in the middle of it all.

PROFÍT. To be a direct line for hurting families.

THE BARBER. Ah, a concerned citizen.

PROFÍT. Thank you, Curtis.

THE BARBER. *(Aside.)* A smart business woman.

PROFÍT. Then let us change The Oblong.

THE BARBER. I gotta go Madam Pro-fee. I can't afford the time for something like you're proposin'. I'm losing heads to you everyday. One by one the kids fall, as does my bank account.

> **(THE BARBER** *starts to leave, but stops.)*

Oh, and also, this play is not about you or me. It's her story. The one you just kicked out.

PROFÍT. Her story?

> *(Blackout.)*

Scene One

(December 14. An **OLD TEACHER**, *when presented with a plant, no matter it an orchid or a daisy, nurtures them just the same.)*

(A high school gym. A fight suddenly breaks out. **TWO BALL PLAYERS** *are at each other's throats, while* **PLAYER 3** *cheers it on. An* **OLD TEACHER** *rushes into the middle of it.)*

OLD TEACHER. Break it up! Break...it... You break it up!

*(***KARMA*** rushes in recording the fight on her phone. The fight is heated.)*

KARMA. Oh shit! Oh shit!

OLD TEACHER. Stop it I said! Come on! Don't just watch! Help!

(The other boy tries to pull the fighters apart.)

Just what happened here? What's goin' on here? Huh? Speak up!

PLAYER 1. That nigga fouled me!

PLAYER 2. Fuck you! I ain't done shit!

PLAYER 1. You did. I was up for the shot –

PLAYER 2. Well you was on my ass the whole time!

PLAYER 1. You talkin' bull nigga!

PLAYER 3. That ain't what had happened. He didn't foul him. It was 'cause –

OLD TEACHER. Slow down! Slow down! One person at a time. Who started it?

PLAYER 1 & 2. He did.

PLAYER 2. It wasn't me man! I was pushed!

PLAYER 1. That nigga started it, and you fuckin' know it! He fuckin' fouled me!

*(***PLAYER 1*** shoves ***PLAYER 2.***)*

OLD TEACHER. Whoa, whoa! That's it. Game over. Everybody home! Give me the ball. What's the matter with you guys? We're officially done for the day.

PLAYER 3. For what?

OLD TEACHER. For what? I have a headache. Let's go.

PLAYER 3. Damn man.

PLAYER 2. The fuck.

OLD TEACHER. Home! Leave! All of you!

> *(The* **BALL PLAYERS** *begrudgingly exit. The* **OLD TEACHER** *catches* **KARMA** *taping.* **KARMA** *puts the phone away.)*

Do you know how wrong that is?

KARMA. That shit was funny as Hell! "Break it up! Break it up!" You got that deep bass for an old dude. For real!

OLD TEACHER. You can leave too.

KARMA. I ain't here to be ballin' teach.

OLD TEACHER. What?

KARMA. You put this up?

> *(She presents the flyer to him.)*

OLD TEACHER. I...yes... I did... Do I know you?

KARMA. Ain't a nigga up in The Oblong don't know me, bruh.

OLD TEACHER. But have I taught you?

KARMA. Look, I'm tryin' to find out about T.

OLD TEACHER. I'll get you a chair. We'll sit. I'm sorry for my outburst. This job steals your sunny beams.

> *(He brings her a chair.)*

You sure I haven't taught you? Aiesha, right? Is it Aiesha?

KARMA. Name's Karma.

> *(She sits. The chair breaks.)*

The fuck, man.

OLD TEACHER. Could have sworn I fixed – I'm so sorry. I'll get you another.

KARMA. I'll stand. Damn.

OLD TEACHER. Gotta fix everything in this school.

KARMA. Except chairs?

OLD TEACHER. The budget they say. "Can't do repairs now, Mr. Meyerson," they say. Or, "Tomorrow, Mr. Meyerson. They're coming tomorrow." I'd have better luck with my super. Look at this gym. It's in shambles. Whole school is.

KARMA. Place's a dump.

OLD TEACHER. Yes, Andre. You / look around –

KARMA. Karma. Not Andre, man.

OLD TEACHER. Did I not call you... I'm sorry... Karma... Karma, Karma, Karma... But if you look around, you can see spray paint residue. See there? And there. / I cleaned it. No one else would.

KARMA. Daaaamn...

OLD TEACHER. Even on the back of the scoreboard. I disciplined a student. So...of course... You see on the scoreboard? That's a penis.

KARMA. Brought the streets to the classroom.

OLD TEACHER. I make do with what I got. That's most schools in The Oblong. Humid in the summer, freezing in the winter, and the children suffer. I'm sure you know how it is.

KARMA. What I know?

OLD TEACHER. Well you've been one of my students here, right?

KARMA. Ain't been in school since the third grade.

OLD TEACHER. Not surprising, I guess.

KARMA. Yo, I'm tryin' to talk to you / 'bout T.

OLD TEACHER. Sorry to confuse you. So many students in my forty years. They all just blend together. Can't tell you how many times... "Mr. Meyerson, that's not my name."

KARMA. Has T turned up yet?

OLD TEACHER. Oh, yes – poor boy. Nope he hasn't. Poor boy. It's been two months.

KARMA. Two months?

OLD TEACHER. No. Longer?

KARMA. Don't ask me.

OLD TEACHER. Don't know. Lose track. Three – four months? Not that long.

KARMA. Seems you hittin' the bottle too much, teach.

OLD TEACHER. And he was doin' so well. Hard working. Driven. Was turning his life around.

KARMA. He was comin' like that?

OLD TEACHER. I created a program here. A place for teens to come. Be constructive. I tutor for the GED, and Terrell was here all the time. Like clockwork. And then...he stopped...

KARMA. And no niggas doin' shit?

OLD TEACHER. He's a friend?

KARMA. He was...my foster brother for a little while.

OLD TEACHER. And this is news to you?

KARMA. We ain't been talkin'...

OLD TEACHER. Oh, I see...

KARMA. Had a disagreement. It's fuckin'...whatever...

OLD TEACHER. How'd you find a flyer, anyway?

KARMA. Ain't seen him for-fuckin-ever, and I'm just walkin', just chillin' in the hood, and then boom I see it on a stop sign, and I like stop, right?

OLD TEACHER. Right.

KARMA. And I'm like, "What. The. Fuck." Had to check all the funeral spots first, 'fore I come here. I know what goes down in this hood.

OLD TEACHER. Surprised you found one.

(He finds a folder filled with papers. Hands it to her.)

OLD TEACHER. Everyone I put up, someone takes it down. Seems you're lucky.

KARMA. What...

OLD TEACHER. Beats me. Find 'em in the garbage torn up.

KARMA. That's fuckin' weird...

OLD TEACHER. You're telling me.

KARMA. And the police? What they doin'?

OLD TEACHER. Have I been questioned? No. Have his friends here been interrogated? Not surprising, not a bit. Sometimes I wonder if she even reported it.

KARMA. She?

OLD TEACHER. Oh. His foster mother. Whom I've never met. Not surprising either. I'm the one puttin' up those flyers. Last week I started that, and how long has he been missing?

KARMA. You know how I can reach her?

OLD TEACHER. Good luck! I've tried. Maybe you'll have better luck. I'll write it down.

> *(He does so.)*

Good luck to you. I hope you find him. I've seen it so often. If I had to guess, what I have to offer is not as attractive as the alternative.

KARMA. What's that mean?

OLD TEACHER. Every one of my students walk to school because busing isn't in the budget, and on their way they pass through a war zone. Block after block of their peers promising them something I can't give them; family, money in their pockets, shelter from the storm. Southside gang. North End Crew. They choose their sides, and...not surprising. Telvin, just like you, I'm afraid, has given up his future.

KARMA. Terrell.

OLD TEACHER. Terrell. Yes. What did I say?

> *(**KARMA** pulls out a notepad, and begins to write.)*

KARMA. Mr. Meyerson, right? How you spell it?

OLD TEACHER. What are you doing?

KARMA. Every nigga that's ever crossed me I write their name down. This pad, got every foster mom, dad, old teacher, random dudes in the street ra-ra-ra. How you spell it?

OLD TEACHER. For what, young lady?

KARMA. To remember. To one day make you remember, understand?

OLD TEACHER. Well get in line –

KARMA. His name's Terrell. Terrell. You spelled his name wrong on the fuckin' flyer!

OLD TEACHER. I did? / No, I...

KARMA. And if I hear one more teacher talkin' 'bout the mothafuckin' future. You really think I'm thinkin' 'bout the future? I'm fuckin' wonderin' if there's a bed open in the shelter tonight.

OLD TEACHER. Well, I'm sorry to hear that...

KARMA. I been a foster kid most my life, teach. Spit from the womb to CPS, to foster home, to foster home, to streets, to shelter, to fuckin' streets again. I don't fuckin' know where I'll be tomorrow. School's the last shit I'm thinkin' about.

OLD TEACHER. That is not at all surprising. You haven't had the right supports. The right teacher I bet.

KARMA. What?

OLD TEACHER. Yeah. Willing to bet. Not surprising. Not at all.

KARMA. Really? Really, teach.

OLD TEACHER. Yeah. As much as I tell myself, "It isn't true, Mr. Meyerson," it always seems to be. You are a product of terrible teachers. Terrible homes. And I'm sorry Katrina. / So sorry.

KARMA. You know what? Fuck you. You ain't shit.

OLD TEACHER. Excuse me. I ain't what?

KARMA. Don't think I stuttered teach. You ain't shit. I ain't so uneducated that I can't write it down for you.

OLD TEACHER. Don't you talk to me that way. "I ain't...poop."

KARMA. Then remember my fuckin' name!

OLD TEACHER. Don't talk to me that way. I am an adult!

KARMA. And I ain't?

OLD TEACHER. Do you know how long I've been teaching – lifting people like you? How long I've been in this place!

KARMA. Hundred years?

OLD TEACHER. Forty years! Way back when my students were white. And I'm not being racist right now. That's a fact. But all my colleagues left. I stayed, despite the loss of funding. Despite the change of neighborhood. Mr. Meyerson stayed.

KARMA. Okay.

OLD TEACHER. "You ain't –" don't say that to me!

KARMA. Whatever.

OLD TEACHER. No freedom, no class small enough, no staff big enough! Forty years! Been cussed out. Been threatened by students, by parents. Been kicked in the balls! I've been to fudgin' therapy! And you say that to me. Tell me "I ain't poop." "I ain't poop"? Mrs. Meyerson hardly sees me, I'm here so much. Most the supplies you see here? Mine. Most the repairs? Mine too. They're gonna have to name the fuckin' school after me, because I am every inch of this place! Every square inch!!

>   (**KARMA**'s been laughing. She finds his outburst funny.)

The Hell is so funny? What the Hell is so funny?

KARMA. "My name is Mr. Meyerson and I ain't poop!"

>   (The **OLD TEACHER** fights the urge to laugh himself.)

OLD TEACHER. Nihilist.

KARMA. Okay. Whatever that means.

OLD TEACHER. Exactly. Are we finished...

KARMA. Karma.

OLD TEACHER. Yes. Karma.

KARMA. Peace.

(She goes.)

OLD TEACHER. Every square inch. Oh, boy...

(He chuckles. Blackout.)

Scene Two

(**KARMA** *meets a strange sort of young gentleman and his hawkish foster mother.*)

(*A. December 15.*)

(*Night time. A pay phone is on the stage.* **KARMA** *works her way through the audience.*)

KARMA. (*To audience.*) Yo, my man. Can you help me out? Lookin' for change.

(*She waits for an answer. She shows her cell to someone else.*)

Out of minutes. Change? Tryin' to call my mom. She's worried 'bout me.

(*She waits for an answer.*)

Hey my lady, I'm one quarter away from a burger. Gladly pay you Tuesday for a burger today. Ha! Just playin'!

(*If she does get change, she might say, "Thanks my nigga. You know what they say's the best nation in the world? Dough-nation!" But if she doesn't, "Ya'll lucky I found a quarter in my pocket!"*)

Been askin' for change all night. Ya'll some stingy mothafuckas, damn! Just playin'. I'm just playin'. Ya'll so serious!

(**KARMA** *makes her way through the crowd to the pay phone, picks up the receiver, drops a coin in the slot pulls a piece of paper from her pocket, and dials. She waits.* **DANTE** *appears, holding a house phone. It rings. He addresses the audience.*)

DANTE. Dante is twelve years old. As you can see, I am not twelve. I am a full grown adult. And this is on purpose... For a point...

(He answers the phone with his best child-like voice.)

DANTE. ... Hello...

KARMA. Oh, sup? Hi. How you? Hello?

DANTE. Who is this?

KARMA. Karma. Hol' up. How old are you? Kinda late, dude.

DANTE. She's not home.

KARMA. Ya foster mom –

DANTE. I'm waitin' for her.

KARMA. Bedtime's for pussies, am I right –

DANTE. She's not home.

KARMA. That's cool. We can chat though. I'm friends with Terrell. He's my boy. Like my brother, understand? Found out he was gone, hit me like a ton of bricks... Ton of bricks. You feel me? You his foster brother?

DANTE. Don't tell her I answered. Please. It's late. She'll be mad.

KARMA. Naw man. My word. I got you. We ain't got to tell. What's your name –

*(**DANTE** hangs up.)*

Hello? Hello...

(She hangs up.)

Fuck, man...

(B. December 16.)

*(An apartment. **KARMA** presses a buzzer. **DANTE** shyly reveals himself. There's an overhead projector in the room.)*

Mail man, lil' G! Just playin'. Caught the mail man at the door, thought I'd be the helpful nigga.

(She hands him the mail. He doesn't accept it.)

KARMA. Sup, dude? Remember my voice? Why you hang up on me yesterday? I was like, "Wow, it's like that?" Had to use the white pages and shit. Put in that detective work, for real.

> *(He doesn't say anything.)*

Where the cat at?

DANTE. Cat?

KARMA. He speaks! Well, damn. Thought I had to find the cat that ate your tongue, you understand?

> *(He just stares at her.)*

Foster mom home?

DANTE. Sleepin'.

KARMA. Okay, okay. Like one in the p.m. She sleepin' like that?

> *(He doesn't say anything.)*

Can I wait for her?

> *(**DANTE** steps inside. **KARMA** enters behind. He sits cross-legged coloring a piece of paper on the floor.)*

So what's up? What's the deal partna?

So... You T's new brother, huh? You two dudes got on? T's a knucklehead, but he's cool...

...okay...

> *(**DANTE** just colors away. **KARMA** is at a loss.)*

Guess, I'll just shut the fuck up, then...

> *(She becomes restless.)*

Look dude, I wanted to talk about Terrell. I been lookin' all over the place for him. Nobody knows shit!

> *(**DANTE** shoves a page aside, and starts another.)*

What you drawin'?

> *(He takes a moment to finish. Hands her the drawing. Turns on the projector.)*

Put it on?

DANTE. Face up.

KARMA. Okay. You just all bizz-nass.

> *(They look at* **DANTE***'s drawing.)*

This your work, little man?

> *(***DANTE*** nods.)*

Who's the man in this?

DANTE. My dad. My real dad. He cleaned schools and stuff.

KARMA. What's them orange things on him?

DANTE. That's just fire. He got robbed and some men lit him on fire.

KARMA. *(Under her breath.)* What the fuck?

DANTE. You a Christian?

KARMA. Nah...

DANTE. You got a cross on.

KARMA. ... Guess I do...

DANTE. So you a Christian.

KARMA. All that salvation crap sounds nice. Sounds good if it was true. Seen too much shit to think there's some nigga in the clouds waitin' on us to thank him, before he gives you shit.

DANTE. God. Is real.

KARMA. Okay.

DANTE. It's true.

KARMA. Okay. Sorry man.

DANTE. Then how you think all this happened?

KARMA. All what happened?

DANTE. The world. How did the world begin? Where we come from?

KARMA. Really? You askin' me that, right now?

> *(He just looks at her.)*

How 'bout I don't fuckin' know. How 'bout that? And to add to that "I don't know," who the fuck cares?

DANTE. It has to be real!

(Beat.)

KARMA. Okay. Damn. It's real.

(He exits. He soon returns with a folder. Hands it to **KARMA**.*)*

DANTE. Every time I clap, you put the next drawing on.

KARMA. You think I be takin' orders lil' man?

(He claps. **KARMA** *quickly places the first sheet on the projector.)*

(It reads, "DANTE'S SECRET STORIES.")

(He claps.)

(A child-like drawing of people praying. A palace on fire and demons with wings circling. Angels cower behind buildings, and street lamps.)

DANTE. Everybody thought God was dead. The demons had taken Heaven and the angels hid themselves in the dark corners of the city. And so The Oblong was in chaos.

*(***DANTE*** claps.)*

(A drawing of kids with guns. The word "BLAM" sparks from their gun barrels, as well as bullets. People cower and the shooters laugh.)

There's a lot of killing going on, and the kids were the reason why. To survive the streets of The Oblong you cannot be afraid of the gun, and you better pray to God or something that you don't see "The Crying Woman."

(He claps.)

(A picture of a pale lady with red tears sprouting from her black eyes.)

(He claps again.)

*(The drawing of a hovering UFO. Angels
hide under sewer grates and behind trees.
A refrigerator, with its door open, has evil
eyes emanating from it. Demons dance and
frolic. Children shoot their guns.)*

God wasn't dead, just depressed by what he saw. He
left us all on a UFO to God knows where. The angels
were too weak, too defeated to protect the innocent
ones. The demons were now free to sneak into our
world through refrigerators, mirrors and closets. And
they would make the children change, join a gang. And
do such bad things.

(He claps.)

*(A drawing of a man riddled with bullet
holes.)*

(He claps.)

*(A drawing of a stick figure choking another
stick figure.)*

(He claps again.)

*(A drawing of a child-like demon face, with a
set of prominent horns.)*

They would do all types of things they normally
wouldn't do. The worst to grab their guns and shoot
each other, over North End or Southside, over revenge,
or nothing at all.

(He claps.)

*(A drawing of a pale white woman in a black
and white dress. The same bloody tears pour
from her black eyes.)*

It was the cry of the dying that fed her. The cry of
the dying that made her look for it more. If she ever
appeared to a kid, her black dress blowing when there
wasn't any wind, her tears like blood, you would know
you were next. And that put the kids on edge. Her name

was Mary, Mary who lost her child by God himself. So she wants revenge on the children of God. A hatred she has so strong, that Satan is afraid of her. Bloody Mary he calls her. The same Mary who named her son Jesus.

(*He claps.*)

(*A drawing of a woman on her knees before a giant cross. Tears pour from her eyes, for the body nailed to it.*)

That's it. That's all. Haven't finished. You can turn it off.

KARMA. Nah, lil' man. Leave it on. I like it. It's cool. Fucked up. But cool. Bloody Mary? Jesus' mother. That shit's deep.

DANTE. You like it?

KARMA. Yeah man. See the world through your eyes and shit.

DANTE. God is real. He just ran away. Why nobody see him anymore.

KARMA. You show T this?

DANTE. I never see him. He was always out. His friends were more important.

KARMA. Nah man. I know T. I'm sure he dug you.

DANTE. How you know?

KARMA. No disrespect, but he loved him some weirdos. For real! He looked up to the craziest dudes. Roughest times in my life? He was there, every time...

(*A long beat.*)

DANTE. His friend got shot.

KARMA. Shot.

DANTE. Terrell's friend.

KARMA. Wait – what?

DANTE. Killed. He saw it. Pickin' me up from school.

KARMA. His friend got *shot*?

DANTE. They just shot him. Everybody was runnin'. There was like four...five shots. And Marlon – Terrell's friend – turn around...

KARMA. Who the Hell shot him?

DANTE. People sayin' it gang stuff. His friend was in a gang.

KARMA. All this happen before he left?

DANTE. Yeah. Like weeks before. That was his best friend. And he saw it... I saw it... There was blood on my face... A lot... Keep thinkin' 'bout...

KARMA. Damn, dude. You can't be thinkin' on that too much, you'll bug the fuck out. Understand? Just try and forget about it. Whatever it takes, understand? It's what I do.

DANTE. You can forget?

KARMA. I did –

FOSTER MOM. *(Offstage.)* What's all this hemmin'-and-hawin' goin' on down there?!

> (**KARMA** *stands to attention.* **DANTE** *grabs her.*)

DANTE. She tells stories.

KARMA. Your foster mom.

DANTE. Uh-huh.

FOSTER MOM. *(Offstage.)* DANTE!

DANTE. She acts. She can be real nice, but she's mean.

FOSTER MOM. *(Offstage.)* You hear me callin' you? Dante!

KARMA. She beat you?

> *(Beat.)*

FOSTER MOM. *(Offstage.)* DANTEEE!!!

KARMA. What about Terrell? What she do to him?

DANTE. Terrell was high a lot.

KARMA. Like weed?

DANTE. No worse. She would...

> *(The* **FOSTER MOM** *enters. She's slovenly and in her sixties.)*

FOSTER MOM. Dante. Do you hear me callin'... Who the Hell are you? What are you doin' in my house?

KARMA. I'm Karma.

FOSTER MOM. Karma.

KARMA. Friend of Terrell's.

FOSTER MOM. Friend?

KARMA. He was my foster brother.

FOSTER MOM. Was.

KARMA. What I said.

FOSTER MOM. You ain't lyin'?

KARMA. Then I'm dyin'.

(Beat. The **FOSTER MOM** becomes more social.)

FOSTER MOM. Terrell. I miss him. We just miss him. Please, have a seat. Sit down. Dante? Your room please.

(**DANTE** goes.)

KARMA. 'Member what I told you.

FOSTER MOM. He hardly remembers what I tell him.

KARMA. He cool.

FOSTER MOM. All I got now. Such a horrible feelin', when somebody's missing. It's like you're stuck and you're everywhere at the same time. Can't think 'bout nothin' but that...thing.

KARMA. Just wonderin', if you've heard anything?

FOSTER MOM. Have you?

KARMA. Nope.

FOSTER MOM. Everybody tellin' me he's a runaway. Nothin' happened to him – you'll never guess what a friend of mine said.

KARMA. What she say?

FOSTER MOM. "I know you hurtin'," she say, "But what about Dante? 'Sides, you could get another." You believe that? Get another. Like he a toy I left at a place or somethin'. Believe that?

KARMA. That's fucked up –

FOSTER MOM. It is fucked up! I told her to get the fuck out. I mean, he may not be my blood, but he's my son. My son. I made a home for him and Dante.

KARMA. Yup.

FOSTER MOM. And it just kills me inside. I have to live with this.

KARMA. You know how long he's been missin'?

FOSTER MOM. Do I know? What kind of dumb question is that child?

KARMA. You ain't got to be defensive. Just askin' how long / he's been gone.

FOSTER MOM. I'm not defensive... The middle of October.

KARMA. Couple of months.

FOSTER MOM. Aren't you smart.

(**KARMA** *shows her the flyer.*)

KARMA. You seen this flyer Foster Moms?

FOSTER MOM. Yeah. I have.

KARMA. Seems somebody's takin' 'em down as soon as they put up.

FOSTER MOM. What?

KARMA. That's what I said. It's like somebody don't want him found.

FOSTER MOM. Who?

KARMA. Been to his program. T's after school shit.

FOSTER MOM. You have.

KARMA. Yeah. I been lookin' all over. Spoke with his teach.

(*Beat.*)

FOSTER MOM. What he say? What that...gentleman say?

KARMA. Mr...

(*She checks her notepad.*)

Meyerson?

FOSTER MOM. Yes. Yes. What did he say?

(*Beat.*)

KARMA. He seemed kinda suspicious of you.

FOSTER MOM. What? He thinks I'm the one takin' them flyers down?

KARMA. Don't know. Seem like to him, you ain't reported T missin'.

FOSTER MOM. Well, he's tellin' you stuff – oh, he thinks I did somethin'? Is that it? To Terrell?

KARMA. Look. I don't know. I don't wanna get caught up in that he-said-she-said shit, okay? 'Cause at the end of the day, who am I to judge, understand? I just came here hopin' to hear some good news.

FOSTER MOM. I'm tired. Is that everything? Need help with anything else?

KARMA. Nope. I'm good.

(**KARMA** *starts to leave.*)

FOSTER MOM. Good.

KARMA. Oh! Your mail.

(**KARMA** *pulls out an envelope.*)

Thought I'd bring it in. Just a lil' lookin' out for T's Foster Mom, ya know what I'm sayin'?

(**KARMA** *hands her the mail.*)

FOSTER MOM. Thank...you...

KARMA. He's a bank. A check in the mail.

FOSTER MOM. Huh?

KARMA. What Dante is too. Bank. Money. Ya still gettin' checks for Terrell? Livin' the pimp life. Huh?

FOSTER MOM. If you think just because some nosey-ass teacher and some fuckin' check in the mail makes me the bad guy you can get the Hell outta my house!

KARMA. I was just sayin' –

FOSTER MOM. I reported him. I went to the police.

KARMA. Okay –

FOSTER MOM. And they just nodded their heads. Scribbled on some paper, told me he a runaway, he's a shelter kid. Told me that's what they do. And sent me on my mothafuckin' way! I turn on the TV last night, and the news yappin' their gums 'bout some little white girl, outside The Oblong – outside I'm telling you. And

I see the parents cryin' and pleadin', makin' themselves heard in front of millions of viewers, and I can't even shout outside my block! And you wanna know why?

KARMA. Why?

FOSTER MOM. 'Cause he's an alien.

KARMA. What?

FOSTER MOM. A mothafuckin' alien! Like he got tentacles and green skin!

KARMA. Lady is you serious right now?

FOSTER MOM. I'm sayin' outside The Oblong! He's familiar to us. He's family. Outside The Oblong he's like a dead cat in the driveway. Just a sad thing. Poor fuckin' cat! Shouldn't been creepin' 'round the car.

Come to my house accusin' me. You want answers. Some nigga to blame. Ask his old girlfriend. Ask her. She and her new nigga was always pushin' his buttons, makin' him nervous. She got dudes followin' him from work, from fuckin' school!

KARMA. His old girlfriend...

FOSTER MOM. There's still little assholes ringin' my buzzer, askin' for Terrell. Tried to tell the police.

KARMA. What you think they want?

FOSTER MOM. Probably all over that friend who got shot dead. But I'm done with you. It's time for you to go. Got no idea who the Hell you are, ain't heard your name before. Ain't even seen your face and suddenly you some important nigga in his life.

Accusin' me. I took him in. I helped him. I did that! I may not be the best parent in the world, but Dante and Terrell had a place to come home to at night. What have you done for Terrell? Huh? Huh?

(**KARMA** *doesn't have an answer.*)

Exhibit A

(December 16. **MADAM PROFÍT** *apologizes for what you're about to see.)*

*(**MADAM PROFÍT**'s office. She tries to work.)*

PROFÍT. *(To audience.)* Her story. What does he mean it's her story? Curtis. "Her story." Do I not matter as much as she does? Am I not worthy of your sympathies? You sir!

(She picks someone out of the audience. Approaches.)

Look at me. Stare me in the eyes. Stare! Tell me. Can you see it?

(She awaits the answer. She better get it.)

Are you looking hard enough – nevermind! It is pain in my eyes, sir. Pain. I have lived in this world much longer than she, and have seen so many things. Can you not see the weight of the world on my shoulders? Do not assume anything of my affluence. It comes from pain. From struggle. I am the funeral director of Amigone Funeral Home, Inc. The things I see day to day. Am I not sympathetical? "Her story."

I remember, recently, a child spoke with me after a funeral service for his...friend – yes, his best friend. He told me, "I'll see you tomorrow." Another service for his brother. He said it like he was leaving work, and back the first thing in the morning. 8 a.m...

This is my life now. Desensitized to Death. I stare it in the face every single day.

*(**YOUNG WOMAN**, twenty-two, enters. She's frazzled and unkempt.)*

Well, all this talk of death, seems someone's on the precipice.

YOUNG WOMAN. Mrs. Profit?

PROFÍT. Pro-fee! The "o" is an "o" not an "ah" and the "t" is silent.

YOUNG WOMAN. Mrs. Pro-fee –

PROFÍT. And call me Madam.

YOUNG WOMAN. Madam Pro-fee –

PROFÍT. How did you get in here?

YOUNG WOMAN. The door was open, I just –

PROFÍT. Are you begging? Have you come for money? This is not a charity.

YOUNG WOMAN. I need your help.

PROFÍT. Ah, it is money you're seeking.

YOUNG WOMAN. Cremation.

PROFÍT. Do you understand why it's hard for me to take you seriously?

YOUNG WOMAN. No.

PROFÍT. Pardon the phrase. But you look like Hell.

YOUNG WOMAN. I do.

PROFÍT. *(Aside.)* A user I bet. I might have to call the police.

YOUNG WOMAN. I wanna be cremated.

PROFÍT. Oh do you?

YOUNG WOMAN. I ain't got the money for it…

>*(**MADAM PROFÍT** laughs.)*

It's funny?

PROFÍT. Funny? It's absurd what you're askin' of me.

YOUNG WOMAN. If it's the killing that bothers you, I got a plan –

PROFÍT. Plan?

YOUNG WOMAN. Never been so sure of somethin' my whole life, Madam. Makes me smile. Like I finally got some control. / Like I got some –

PROFÍT. Are you talkin' suicide, child? Come on. Out.

YOUNG WOMAN. Please. Please, ma'am.

PROFÍT. None of that. Out. Out!

YOUNG WOMAN. I'm askin' for your sympathy.

(PROFÍT stops.)

PROFÍT. Sympathy?!

(Aside.) She asks for my sympathy.

YOUNG WOMAN. Yes. Please Madam Pro-fee.

PROFÍT. *(Aside.)* My sympathy she asks for, when she's clearly the one to blame for her current position.

YOUNG WOMAN. Please, listen.

PROFÍT. It's my sympathy you want, huh?

YOUNG WOMAN. Yeah.

PROFÍT. *(Aside.)* Just watch how quickly I sum her up.

YOUNG WOMAN. I wish I could pay you, but –

PROFÍT. Life has been hard, has it?

YOUNG WOMAN. Yeah.

PROFÍT. Lack of opportunity.

YOUNG WOMAN. Yeah.

PROFÍT. No parents.

YOUNG WOMAN. A father.

PROFÍT. A father?

YOUNG WOMAN. But he ain't no parent.

PROFÍT. *(Aside.)* Oh, I have her figured.

YOUNG WOMAN. I don't wanna explain myself. Will you cremate –

PROFÍT. And so you're a user.

YOUNG WOMAN. There's more to it.

PROFÍT. Still excusing yourself.

YOUNG WOMAN. Excusin'... / what you mean excusin' –

PROFÍT. *(Aside.)* See her flounder. Next will come her horrible victimhood. It's everybody else's doing. Not her own.

YOUNG WOMAN. I ain't excusin' myself, I just want, what I –

PROFÍT. Can you tell me as someone who has grown up with your same lack of opportunity, lack of parenting, lack of access, how I am where I am and you are where you are?

YOUNG WOMAN. Then you get what I mean –

PROFÍT. No, no. I don't, child.

YOUNG WOMAN. I'll do the thing. Just askin' you to do me the kindness and cremate me. Won't be buried in the earth. It don't want me here.

PROFÍT. Just where do you think ashes end up, child?

YOUNG WOMAN. Please! I'm askin' –

PROFÍT. Black folk don't kill themselves dear. If that were true none of us would be here. There would be no such thing as an African-American. I wouldn't be here. Horrible things happened in my life, but I dealt with it. I took it, and I got right back up again. I ate it. I eat disappointment. Degradation. Downtroddeness. I made it food. It sustains me. We don't kill ourselves.

YOUNG WOMAN. Sister...

PROFÍT. Sister?! You'll have to leave.

(*The* **YOUNG WOMAN** *starts to go. She stops.*)

YOUNG WOMAN. You know what I'm thinkin'?

PROFÍT. (*Aside.*) What could she be thinking?

YOUNG WOMAN. I'm thinkin' I seem a little too familiar to you.

(*She looks to the audience.*)

What ya'll think?

PROFÍT. No, no, no, no! No you don't. You don't get to – you don't get to talk to them. Go. Go!

(**MADAM PROFÍT** *tries to push her out. The* **YOUNG WOMAN** *stops her.*)

I will call the police!

(*The* **YOUNG WOMAN** *goes.*)

And I am not your sister!

(*The* **YOUNG WOMAN** *exits.* **PROFÍT** *takes a moment and addresses the audience.*)

PROFÍT. I'm sorry you had to see that. I'm so sorry. I didn't want you to come all this way to see that. It's obscene. Uncomfortable. Upsetting. I'm just tired of having to apologize. I promise there is more to us than that. She is in no way representative of our depth, of our diversity, our facility to strive. To adapt. Oh, I will show you my place in this play. When next you see me, you will see my talent at work.

(Blackout.)

Scene Three

(December 17. **KARMA** *and* **TERRELL'S EX-GIRLFRIEND** *sing the jealousy duet.)*

(On the streets. **THE EX**, *a young black mother, sits cross-legged behind a sign that reads, "MAMA SAID THERE'D BE DAYS LIKE THIS." Her stroller with child is close by. The baby can't be seen.* **KARMA** *enters, much to* **THE EX***'s chagrin.)*

THE EX. Fuuuck, man! / Shit!

KARMA. Hey lady –

THE EX. Don't even, yo. Don't fuckin' / even!

KARMA. You still couch surfin' with a muthafuckin' baby?

THE EX. Keep walking dick hole!

KARMA. Dick hole?

THE EX. Bitch, did I stutter?

KARMA. Your words got distorted by your cat breath.

THE EX. You don't even make fuckin' sense, yo.

KARMA. That your breath smells like a cat's?

THE EX. Bye.

KARMA. Na, na, na. You pushin' a stroller though?

THE EX. Go fuck yourself!

KARMA. Who the daddy? / And you askin' for money?

THE EX. We ain't friends, bitch.

KARMA. Is that...

THE EX. Don't... Yo, don't you fuckin' say it –

KARMA. Holy fuck! It's his? That baby's Terrell's –

THE EX. It's not his fuckin' baby!

(The baby starts crying.)

KARMA. I don't know my nigga. You seem pretty guilty.

THE EX. It's not his fuckin' baby! That jealous mothafucka!

KARMA. Jealous?

THE EX. Yeah, fuckin' jealous! Why my baby father's in jail, 'cause he kep' on sweatin' me!

KARMA. Wait. What the fuck are you talkin' about?

THE EX. Not your problem. Not your problem, boo.

KARMA. The fuck it is. T's missin'! You know that?

THE EX. What?

KARMA. He just vanished, understand?

THE EX. When?

KARMA. Don't fuckin' know.

THE EX. I hope them niggas got him.

KARMA. Hope who got him –

THE EX. Terrell saw us in the street, yo. Shoutin' 'bout his friend. Houndin' my man. Out his head, yo.

KARMA. His friend.

THE EX. T jumped him. And now my man's in jail!

KARMA. When did that happen?

THE EX. You wanna fuckin' date?

KARMA. That's what, "When did that happen?" means.

THE EX. October! Our anniversary, yo. And T knew it! Fuckin' wilin' out on some shit.

KARMA. He jumped him? Hell naw!

THE EX. T's got niggas fienin' for him, yo. He show his face Southside...

KARMA. Your man in a crew?

THE EX. Ain't tellin' you shit.

KARMA. He was yellin' 'bout his friend?

THE EX. Get out my face, yo.

KARMA. Wait. You know 'bout his friend?

THE EX. Ain't sayin' shit.

KARMA. Fuck! Your man shot T's friend.

THE EX. He ain't shot that nigga, yo! It was...

(She stops herself.)

KARMA. You know who shot him?

(**THE EX** *doesn't answer.*)

KARMA. Shiiiit. You do. / You do.

THE EX. I ain't sayin' shit, yo!

KARMA. It was your man's crew. And T knew it.

THE EX. Shut the fuck up. I ain't tole you nothin'!

KARMA. Why you such a bad liar? You crackin' under pressure?

(**THE EX** *pushes her.*)

THE EX. Shut the fuck up. You ain't gettin' shit from me, horse face.

KARMA. Maybe I choke the rest out of you.

THE EX. Go 'head, yo.

KARMA. I ought to pop you in your fuckin' mouth.

(**THE EX** *gets in* **KARMA**'s *face.*)

THE EX. Go 'head! Go 'head bitch!

KARMA. I will!

THE EX. Fuck Terrell and fuck you, you fuckin' dyke bitch!

KARMA. *(To audience.)* Imma have to apologize for the shit you 'bout to see right now. Had it been my way, things woulda ended up different. If I could like grab time and fuckin' like yank it backwards, I would, you know? But that ain't how The Oblong works. It's hurt-sport. I ain't afraid to fight. And I fight dirty. Only stupid people believe in a fair fight. So when it comes to hurt-sport, you better hurt the other person real quick, understand?

My advice to all ya'll? Just focus on Terrell. Everything else is some bullshit.

> *(And so they fight. And it is vicious. They slam into the stroller. It rolls a little. The baby cries. The cries underscore the grunts and shouts of the intense wrestle. Clothes are torn. A nose is bloodied. And the baby still cries.* **KARMA**'s *losing, so she pulls out a brick.)*

What bitch. What?

THE EX. A brick. You got a fuckin' brick?

KARMA. Come up on me!

THE EX. Yo! You fucked up!

KARMA. I don't even like you!

THE EX. Shut the fuck up!

KARMA. Watch your baby, yo!

> (**THE EX** *rocks the baby carriage. It doesn't seem to work.*)

THE EX. You're fuckin' crazy! Do you even remember what you did to Terrell, yo?

KARMA. Don't start that shit –

THE EX. No you don't.

KARMA. 'Course I fuckin' –

THE EX. You fuckin' stole from the fosters he was stayin' with, yo! He got kicked out a place he liked!

KARMA. That was revenge! Revenge! He straight forgot about me!

THE EX. Oh my God! Do you hear yourself? / Do you even –

KARMA. It was all about you / 'cause you put out real quick!

THE EX. Them fosters thought he was stealin' from 'em, yo – what you mean I put out quick?

KARMA. You heard me!

THE EX. You're outta your fuckin' mind yo! He hated you after that shit! Hated –

KARMA. No, he didn't –

THE EX. He told you to your face, yo! Got abandonment issues and shit.

KARMA. Abandonment issues? Fuck! You the ho cryin' whenever he wanted to hang with me.

THE EX. Ya lyin'!

KARMA. Pullin' at his clothes. "Please Terrell! / Please!"

THE EX. Can't believe he told you that! Fuck that nigga!

KARMA. Quit sayin' that! He's fuckin' family! Only family I got!

THE EX. Well you been disowned!

KARMA. Ain't the fuckin' point. I'm lookin' for Terrell...

THE EX. What even makes you think he'll look for you, you go missin'?

> *(Beat.)*

KARMA. ... He would...

THE EX. Shut the fuck up, he would.

KARMA. This is hard to say, but you know him better than I do. He was your boyfriend.

THE EX. Only when we was fuckin'. Nigga got a rock heart.

KARMA. Regardless of what he done, or how you feel about him, understand? Regardless, regardless, regardless. He's people. At the end of the day he's a person. A human fuckin' being. And he's gone.

THE EX. He and I got a history, yo. That shit ain't changin'!

KARMA. If you know anything. Anything. I ain't got much to go on.

> *(Beat.)*

THE EX. Don't fuckin' care.

KARMA. Why it feel like I'm the only nigga lookin' for him?

THE EX. You serious right now?

KARMA. The only nigga who gives a fuck!

THE EX. Because you are.

KARMA. He's my brother.

THE EX. Then you better find him real quick.

> **(THE EX** *takes up her stroller.)*

Bye.

> **(THE EX** *exits.)*

Exhibit B

(December 20. Just as she promised earlier, **MADAM ROSE PROFÍT** *shows you her talent.)*

(A viewing room. A casket is brought in. It's open. **MADAM PROFÍT** *addresses the crowd. She reads from a paper.)*

PROFÍT. My name is Madam Rose Profít. The "o" is an "o" not an "ah" and the "t" is silent. Pro-fee. And I want to thank you all for being here. For bearing witness to something a mother should never have to face. The murder of a child. The loss of Joshua.

THE MOTHER. *(From somewhere.)* Jamal.

PROFÍT. I would like to recognize the family, the friends, acquaintances, and concerned members of the community, who support this devastated mother, by being witness to her grief. It was my idea and I very much insisted that the service be open casket. I also advised this dear mother to leave her precious child, Joshua, as she found him.

THE MOTHER. Jamal.

PROFÍT. Sorry. It's my writing. Terrible penmanship. I was in a rush. Where was I...? Yes! His face bloodied and bruised by gang violence, a child gone missing. Missing for months, like so many of our young, only to be found a victim of a pointless scuffle. Let me show you the struggles of our community, on the contours of this child's ruined face. Now let us focus on this young man, Jamal – Joshua...

(She opens her Bible. She checks her watch. She flies through the verses.)

John Chapter 14: Verse 1–6. "Do not let your hearts be troubled. Trust in God, trust also in me. In my Father's house are many rooms, if it were not so I would have told you. I'm going there to prepare a place for you. And if I go and prepare a place for you, I will come back

and take you to be with me that you also may be where
I am. You know the way to the place where I am going."
Later he says, "I am the way and the truth and the life.
No one comes to the Father except through me."

Now usually I would say a bit about the deceased, but
time is very tight today. We do not have very long, and
I apologize, but we were booked solid this weekend.
But before we open the floor, I will end by saying...
Death is only a crossing. It is not an ending. We will all
see each other again in God's glorious kingdom. Now
isn't that something to look forward to? Who would
like to remember Josh... Ja-mal??

> *(A long beat.)*

Anyone... Anyone out there? We have a little time –

THE MOTHER. *(Offstage.)* Me. I will.

PROFÍT. Oh, good.

> (**THE MOTHER** *appears from some place. She's*
> *thirty years old and dressed in the finest she*
> *can afford.* **PROFÍT** *steps aside.)*

THE MOTHER. Thank you... Thank...you... Oh man... I...
Okay, Imma keep it together... My son...my...son...
Jamal. He was a...good... *Everybody* who knew...
him... Fuck! Damn... It just hurts... What was I
going... Everybody who knew him... He was funny,
like... He was, just good... Imma stop. Fuck! The Hell
am I sayin'? I got nothin'. I'm fuckin' diggin' for shit.
There's nothin' to fuckin' say – grieve! There's nothin'
to grieve. Shit. *Fourteen!* FOURTEEN YEARS OLD!!!
A fuckin'...uh, uh...tadpole! A tadpole! Little nigga ain't
even fully formed yet.

PROFÍT. Please. Don't –

THE MOTHER. I got the floor, Pro-*fee*! I ain't finished!

PROFÍT. I understand you're devastated –

THE MOTHER. Anybody else got somethin' to say? Anybody?
What you wanna say that's specific 'bout him? Huh?
Get real specific. And don't lie to me, 'cause I know

what you think. If you saw my boy in the street. If you heard his name, I know exactly what you think. Don't lie.

(She asks someone.)

What about you? Nothin'? Sorry for your goddamn loss? Say you're sorry for my loss. Say it.

(Beat. **MADAM PROFÍT** *interferes in the exchange.)*

PROFÍT. Please... I'm sorry. You don't have to say anything –

THE MOTHER. Say it.

(She waits. Maybe she hears it. She moves on. **PROFÍT** *signals the house lights to come up. They do.)*

What about you? "I'm sorry for your loss." Mean it.

(She waits. She moves on to two more people. **PROFÍT** *urges one of the mourners to attend to* **THE MOTHER.***)*

Say it. "I'm sorry for your loss." I don't believe you. You, lady. "I'm sorry for your loss." Say it...

(The mourner steps in and takes hold of **THE MOTHER.***)*

PROFÍT. Ladies and gentleman, if we can take a break. Just a little break. I'm afraid we've gone just a bit too far. It's time to move the service into the reception space. There are drinks and refreshments. At a cost, of course. Now please do exit. I'm so sorry. You don't have to go home, but you can't... Nevermind.

*(***MADAM PROFÍT** *waits.)*

Go on! Go on, I got other people comin' in. I'm waiting...

*(***MADAM PROFÍT** *waits.)*

ACT II

Scene Four

(December 22. The coal black rooster laments the hot commodity of youth.)

*(An old man, **GOTTO**, sixties, saunters out with a cane which unfolds into a stool. He sits. He smokes a pipe. He stares. B-boy music suddenly blasts from a boom box*. Three of **GOTTO'S BOYS** burst onto the scene. They set up.)*

BOY 2. What time is it?!

(No answer.)

I said... WHAT TIME IS IT?!

*(**GOTTO** gestures to the crowd to respond.)*

WHAT TIME IS IT?!

ALL BOYS. SHOWTIME!!!

BOY 2. Maybe I need to be more specific!

BOY 3. Yeah, boy! More specific!

BOY 2. White people! What time is it?!

ALL BOYS. SHOWTIME!!!

BOY 2. Asian people! What time is it?!

ALL BOYS. SHOWTIME!!!

BOY 2. Latin people! ¿Que hora es?

ALL BOYS. ¡ESPECTACULO!

---

*A license to produce *The Revolving Cycles Truly and Steadily Roll'd* does not include a performance license for any third-party or copyrighted recordings. Licensees should create their own.

BOY 1. Habla espanol.

BOY 2. And black people!!! What time is it?

ALL BOYS. SHOWTIME!!!

> (**GOTTO** *laughs hysterically. The music changes.* **GOTTO'S BOYS** *go off into a sad display of break dancing and flat hat tricks. He watches for a bit. And then...*)

GOTTO. *(To audience.)* Not perfect. Right? You'd think, "Why even do it?" It musn't be perfect, you understand? Talent can open a wallet, sure, but commitment to something bad can be even more rewarding. Empathy is our way. No. I take that back. We don't want your empathy. It's rare anyway. It's your sympathy we want. Your pity. You give so much easier that way. You pay and it keeps us where we are.

> (*There's a shout.* **BOY 2** *has hurt himself. He's down on the ground whimpering at his foot.* **KARMA** *enters with a black eye. She keeps her distance.*)

Enough, enough, babies. Turn it off! Turn it off! Goddammit! I said turn the fuckin' radio off!

> (*They do. Then they're frozen, looking to their fallen comrade.* **GOTTO** *ambles his way over.*)

Too much! Too goddamn much! What the Hell I been tellin' you little shits?

BOY 2. Sorry, Mr. Gotto. I'm sorry.

GOTTO. You're sorry? You're sorry now!

BOY 2. I'm sorry, I'm sorry.

BOY 1. He's alright Mr. Gotto.

GOTTO. How you know that?

BOY 1. He...

GOTTO. Shut the Hell up! You okay boy?

BOY 2. I'm – I'm good.

GOTTO. I took you in, off the streets, but you'll be back real quick. You know that. If you can't pull your weight, can't contribute –

BOY 3. He said he's fine.

GOTTO. Shut the fuck up, I said!

BOY 2. Mr. Gotto. I got this.

GOTTO. Do ya now?

BOY 2. Trust.

GOTTO. Then stand up and walk for old Gotto. Let me see it.

> (**BOY 2** *tries. It's difficult, but he clumsily walks for* **GOTTO**. **GOTTO***'s demeanor becomes lighter.*)

Ahhhh, there you go. You probably bruised it. Get him back home. He'll be fine.

> (*He hugs* **BOY 2**. *Kisses him on the cheek.*)

BOY 2. I'm sorry, Mr. Gotto.

GOTTO. It's okay my babies. Sorry to yell at you in front of an audience. It's unfair to you. You boys are doin' so well, so well.

BOY 3. Mr. Gotto, why don't we put him on a corner. Have him ask for change. People'll feel sorry for him.

GOTTO. Well, goddamn boy, you just might be my favorite. Now go on boys. Earn that paper for old Gotto. And you bring it on back to me. You bring it on back.

> (**GOTTO'S BOYS** *gather themselves and exit.*)

KARMA. What time is it?!

GOTTO. Oh, there she go!

KARMA. That who I think it is?

GOTTO. *There* she go!

KARMA. Gotto?

GOTTO. Who else you see?

KARMA. Aw, man it's just a coal black rooster!

GOTTO. What you mean it's just me?

KARMA. You ain't nobody important!

GOTTO. Don't make me come over there!

KARMA. Keep walkin'!

GOTTO. *You* keep walkin'!

KARMA. You ain't shit!

GOTTO. I come over there and bust your tooth you think me somebody!

KARMA. You gonna bust my tooth? I'll straight box your left nutsack!

(They laugh. It's an old routine.)

GOTTO. You never cease to impress me.

KARMA. I'm impressive.

GOTTO. Im-pre-ssive. You still thievin' for your daily bread?

KARMA. Who wants to know?

GOTTO. When you workin' for me again?

KARMA. You gonna ask me that right now?

GOTTO. I ain't seen you for sometime, girly. You hidin' from me?

KARMA. You a dumb mothafucka. I remember how you do.

GOTTO. What you mean, "How I do"?

KARMA. Nigga you like the big bad wolf and shit.

GOTTO. That's called tough love.

KARMA. Bullshit –

GOTTO. Whoa, whoa. What happened to your face girly?

KARMA. Question should be what happened to the other nigga's face.

*(**GOTTO** stares her down.)*

What? You studyin' me?

GOTTO. Somethin' ain't right... Your tone's all off.

KARMA. Tone.

GOTTO. Yeah...

KARMA. Nigga. Back. Up.

GOTTO. Hungry?

KARMA. Nope.

GOTTO. Here's an energy bar. Go on. May be a month off, but good. Got nutrients for ya.

KARMA. Whatever.

> *(She takes the bar. Starts in on it, like she hasn't eaten for sometime.* **GOTTO** *still stares.)*

What, man? Damn.

GOTTO. It's more than food. Somethin' else.

KARMA. Why you so creepy, Gotto? Man I knew I shouldn't come this way. You the last nigga I wanna see –

GOTTO. Tell ole Gotto. What's on your spirit?

> *(Beat.)*

KARMA. Got any new recruits?

GOTTO. New recruits?

KARMA. Have you picked up any adoptees off the street recently?

GOTTO. Like who?

KARMA. Come on, Gotto.

GOTTO. Quit dancin' round me. What's the point, 'fore I start shoutin' at you.

> *(Beat.)*

KARMA. My foster brother. Been missin' over two months now. Tried all the things. Nothin'.

GOTTO. And so you come to ole Gotto.

KARMA. You know what? Fuck it! Figure it on my own.

GOTTO. 'Course ya will. You're formidable girly. But you came all this way, so...

> *(She shows him the flyer.)*

KARMA. Terrell.

> *(A long beat.)*

Maybe you ain't –

GOTTO. Oh, don't ask me 'bout that boy. Don't you do that.

KARMA. You seen him?

(He just shakes his head.)

GOTTO. Oh, boy. Ohhh, boy. It's a sad thing, Gotto will tell ya. A sad, sad thing.

KARMA. What?

(He takes the flyer.)

GOTTO. Just last month I came across that boy, beggin', beggin' for somethin'. Addicted. A user. Askin' for money, sure, but I saw through that. I knew where the money was goin'.

I seen enough little niggas like him to know it. And he flips me the bird. And I tell him, "I love you." And he give me a look like he ain't heard it before or heard it enough.

"You gonna help me or not?" He said to me, hinting I was wasting his time.

I say it again. Deeply. "I love you, brother. I ain't got no judgments for ya. Tell you what? Come with me and I'll feed your need. We will reduce the harm. And shove out the shame. 'Cause brother it ain't your fault."

"The fuck you talkin' 'bout?" He say to me. His face all discombobulated like I'm lyin' to the brother. "You don't even know me, man."

But that's where he's wrong. I do know him. I know what he's a product of. I told him, "You pushed out into a community of backsides. Understand me? Everywhere you look, it's just people's back. And though they ain't lookin' they got you figured out. Your story's my story."

"Story's called poor choices," he say, sorta jokin'. And I laugh. Poor choices? "Is that what they got you trained to recite?" I ask him. And the user nods like a cop. Then I say, "It's called no choice. It's a disease, to be medicated not incarcerated." And I offered him my hand. And he just looked at it. Couldn't look me in the eye. Shame. Shame they gave him. "I love you. I love you."

I tell him "You're not a percentage or a statistic. You are Terrell. And not any other negro named Terrell. Same letters and junk, but the heart, the spirit of the name is uniquely you. You are a missed opportunity. A commodity."

"A commodity?" he ask. "Somethin' valuable." I say. "I love you." I say it again. Deep. He understood me, then.

And Terrell's face gets all soft. His eyes welled up... So...beautiful – rare. How many times in that boy's life had he the chance to be a child? And he took my hand. I pulled him close, and I held him in my arms.

And we walked The Oblong, all the way to my nest. And what a sight we were, this shrivelled up youth, cryin' desperately in my arms, walking the tough streets of the inner city. Swear the whole world stopped...

> *(He stops. She waits.)*

KARMA. What happened, man?

GOTTO. I don't know what to tell you girly.

KARMA. Just tell it straight. Fuck.

GOTTO. He vanished. No word. Nothin'. Just days after he come.

KARMA. You said this was last month?

GOTTO. Yep. The corner where he slept in my nest? Nowhere to be found that mornin'.

> *(He hands her some things.)*

His cell phone. His wallet. Found it all on his sheets. Boy left without a word. That sound familiar?

> *(She looks at the items.)*

Had to charge the phone. Not many saved numbers. Not many calls made. Well, only saved number was to the Chicken Shack. His wallet still had money in it, his ID. Thought to myself, "Now why would someone with nothin' but the clothes on his back do that? Leave his wallet with twenty-three dollars in it?"

KARMA. Maybe he got found.

GOTTO. Don't sound good. Said he got people lookin' for him.

KARMA. Yup.

> *(Beat.)*

GOTTO. Sorry.

KARMA. It's...

GOTTO. I'll find ya if I hear somethin'. I expect the same from you.

KARMA. You think I'll send him back to you? Nigga, no!

> **(GOTTO** *chortles and goes on about his business.)*

Hey Gotto! Ain't you said his wallet had money in it?

GOTTO. I did.

KARMA. Well, where is it?

GOTTO. In a good place. Catch you on the flip!

> *(He exits.)*

Exhibit C

*(December 22. **MADAM PROFÍT** shares the news, and in doing so finds her place in the play.)*

*(**MADAM PROFÍT** sits. She reads the paper.)*

PROFÍT. You've heard the news? I'm sure you have. What happened at the mall. What happened at the mall, days before Christmas. Just to think about little baby Jesus in a manger those centuries ago, and the generosity of those three wise men. Only to read this morning, days before Christmas... Listen to this.

"A wild flash mob of over 100 crazed teens stormed and trashed a mall on the south side of The Oblong yesterday afternoon. The young teens caused so much damage and hysteria that the shopping center was forced to close before the Christmas holiday." Amazing! Absolutely amazing.

(She spots someone. Gives the paper to them.)

Read that paragraph for me. Go on. Read it out loud. This is your city as well, no matter how you see it.

(The person she asks might not be loud enough. She redirects them.)

(The someone reads, "'I was begging them to stop. There were a lot of kids, hundreds of kids. Security would chase them out one door and they would come back in another door,' said Mohammad Yousuf, clerk at the Candy Shop.")

*(**MADAM PROFÍT** snatches the paper back.)*

That was going on. Our children. They robbed and looted, vandalized and harassed. The paper said there were kids swimming in the fountain, setting pets lose in the pet shop.

These children were stuffing toilets and making them overflow. There were BB guns being shot at unsuspecting individuals. A child was spanking the florist with his own flowers.

The waste. The absolute waste... This is what Curtis meant. Her story! Not "her" singularly. "Her" as in all our youth. It's their story!

Our youth have gone missing. And by that I mean they're nowhere to be found, but jail or on the streets or in my parlor. So few have found their place at the table. But I know where they are. I can finally affirm my place in this play!

(Blackout.)

Scene Five

(**KARMA**'s *taught the parable of the great eye of the inner city.*)

(*A. Christmas Eve.*)

(*It is almost pitch black. We hear indiscernible noises. A flashlight flicks on, and we can make out a figure dressed in what appears to be a fast food uniform, and holding a broom. He removes his hat and an apron.* **THE FRIEND**, *eighteen, eats an apple.*)

(*He sits down on what appears to be a sleeping bag. He suddenly hears a noise.*)

THE FRIEND. Who's there?

(**KARMA** *reveals herself. She carries some large shopping bags.*)

KARMA. Just security. Doin' my rounds.

THE FRIEND. Yo, who the fuck are you?

KARMA. I'm… I'm just…hungry, man. This a Chicken Shack. Just tryin' to get me a thigh and a wing. That's all, man. Can you hook a nigga up?

THE FRIEND. Look man, you got five seconds –

KARMA. Terrell! I'm lookin' for Terrell.

THE FRIEND. … Terrell…

KARMA. Yeah, man. That's it.

THE FRIEND. What make you think I know somethin'?

KARMA. Oh come on man. You know somethin'.

(*Beat.*)

My name is Karma. Used to be his foster sister.

(*Beat.*)

I ain't lyin'.

THE FRIEND. How'd you get in?

KARMA. This nigga right here? A ninja!

THE FRIEND. How'd you get in?

KARMA. Turn the knob. And push. Lock the door, dude. You in the hood.

>   (*Beat.*)

THE FRIEND. What you want?

KARMA. You know where he is?

THE FRIEND. *You* know where he is?

KARMA. You make an awesome parrot. You really sleepin' here?

THE FRIEND. What's your name again?

KARMA. Karma.

THE FRIEND. Why I ain't never heard about you, Karma?

KARMA. You know...family...

THE FRIEND. He talked to me about his family.

KARMA. Maybe he didn't like me too much. But we still family.

>   (*Beat.*)

THE FRIEND. Maybe you come back tomorrow at a decent time. Not one in the fuckin' mornin'.

KARMA. Maybe I will. Then I'll tell your boss-man his employee's sleepin' in a back room after hours. That cool?

THE FRIEND. You don't know shit.

KARMA. Been stakin' the spot. Coupla nights. See you come to work at three. See you and your work peeps out at closin' time. But then all a sudden one in the a.m., there you are, sneakin' on in, and out before sunrise.

THE FRIEND. What you want?

KARMA. I found these.

>   (*She hands him* **TERRELL***'s wallet and cell phone.*)

THE FRIEND. That's his stuff.

KARMA. Yup.

THE FRIEND. How you got all this?

KARMA. You know where he is?

THE FRIEND. I asked you somethin'.

KARMA. You so paranoid, bruh.

THE FRIEND. You the one sneakin' up in here askin' questions.

KARMA. Fuck. He and I, we family. I ain't lyin' to you.

(**THE FRIEND** *waits.*)

You don't know where he at?

THE FRIEND. Nah. Nope.

KARMA. I hope you ain't fuckin' with me.

THE FRIEND. That's the truth, though.

(*Beat.*)

KARMA. Fuck it!

(*She kicks over one of her bags. Stuff scatters everywhere.* **THE FRIEND** *eventually starts to pick stuff up. She joins in.*)

Can I sleep here?

THE FRIEND. What?

KARMA. Can I sleep here? Cold as fuck out there.

THE FRIEND. Are you serious?

KARMA. C'mon man.

THE FRIEND. Why you got all these bags?

KARMA. Christmas tomorrow. Did some holiday shoppin'. Spent all my five fingas! Get it? Five finger discount!

THE FRIEND. Shut up.

KARMA. Want a towel, some nail clippers?

THE FRIEND. Is that all you got?

KARMA. Nigga, don't look a gift horse in the mouth. Here you go. Some deodorant. Merry Christmas.

THE FRIEND. Thanks. You really hungry?

KARMA. Fuck, yeah!

THE FRIEND. You want an apple? I got another.

KARMA. This what you offer a nigga when they in the mothafuckin' Chicken Shack?

THE FRIEND. Shit'll kill you.

KARMA. Shit is food.

THE FRIEND. Whatever. It's gonna be cold.

KARMA. Well, bruh...

THE FRIEND. Don't look a gift horse in the mouth.

> *(He goes out. He comes back in with a to-go box.* **KARMA** *breaks into it. She eats like she hasn't eaten in years.)*

KARMA. Thanks, man.

THE FRIEND. That stuff's vile.

KARMA. You the nigga that works here.

THE FRIEND. Got a record.

> *(**KARMA** laughs.)*

KARMA. Of course.

THE FRIEND. That's funny.

KARMA. Yep.

THE FRIEND. Do you think it's funny – fair when a nigga has served their time, fuckin' out early on parole for good behavior... Supposedly on track to rehabilitation. The fuckin' sign out the prison gate has the word "correctional" on it, like the nigga's been corrected, and he's got to tick a box on a job application asking if he's been convicted of a crime?

KARMA. Don't get hot. It's fuckin' funny.

THE FRIEND. Shut the fuck up.

KARMA. You don't laugh much. Huh?

THE FRIEND. You know what? You know how the police puts those great big lights near the projects, like fuckin', I don't know, like they bottled up the sun and shit? Those fuckin' lights towerin' over the hood or whatever, to spot the bad guys.

KARMA. Yeah.

THE FRIEND. Just tonight, I was walkin', mindin' my business, on my way back to the Chicken Shack. That great fuckin' light beamin' down on me. And up walks Mr. Police Officer.

KARMA. Oh shit.

THE FRIEND. Right behind me, right? Callin' after me. "Yo!" he shoutin'. "Yo!" Like he down or some shit. I turn around, fuckin' pissed, 'cause I know what this is. And he ask me, what I got on me. I tell him, "Nothin'." Mr. Police Officer ask me to put my hands behind my head, and I ask him why. I tell him he needs a reason. He holds out his cuffs. Mr. Police Officer asks me if there's a problem with his request. I'm on fuckin' parole. Can't get arrested. That's jail again. "Put your hands on your head." I'm just thinkin' 'bout sayin' no. I wanna say it. I just wanna fuckin' say it.

KARMA. And you did right? You shouted that shit all gangsta right?

THE FRIEND. That's jail. That's back to prison. Or my life.

KARMA. So you punked out.

THE FRIEND. I put my hands behind my head.

KARMA. You punked out –

THE FRIEND. This shit ain't funny. You know what's happenin' to niggas. Quit stuntin'.

KARMA. I ain't –

THE FRIEND. Listen nigga. He tells me to get on my knees. I ask him why. He doesn't answer. Just waits. He knows I will. I'm starin' at my shadow on the ground, that great big eye of the inner city starin' down on me. This presence, right? You step out the spot or cross the line... They on that perch. Got you in their sights... and... BLAM!

Mr. Police Officer is feelin' me up.

Asks for an apology for ruinin' his holiday. An apology. I do. Say I'm sorry, starin' at my shadow on the fuckin' ground... I said sorry...

(There's only that. The "sorry" floating.)

You know what I remember 'bout my first day locked up?

KARMA. What?

THE FRIEND. Felt...right at home. Them bars. Them walls. That tiny space. Bad food. The fuckin' bed. No money. Them POs shoutin' me down. Knew it all my life. Just wasn't no secret no more...

KARMA. Dude. You need some downward dog, goddamn.

(**THE FRIEND** *bursts into laughter.*)

THE FRIEND. Man, you must've bugged the shit outta Terrell, for real. If people only knew what the fuck happens at a Chicken Shack at two in the mornin'.

KARMA. On Christmas Eve.

THE FRIEND. Christmas Day.

KARMA. Yup. It is.

(*They laugh. It grows quiet again.*)

You think he's dead?

THE FRIEND. Don't know. I tell you what, he didn't want to be found.

KARMA. He say that to you?

THE FRIEND. Yup. He used to pull down all the flyers this old teacher was puttin' up. Them missing posters and shit. He ask me to help him sometimes.

KARMA. ... Shit... When you last seen him?

THE FRIEND. Couple of weeks.

KARMA. Weeks? How many?

THE FRIEND. I don't know. Two. Three?

KARMA. Which one, nigga?

THE FRIEND. I don't know. I told him he can't be comin' 'round no mo'.

KARMA. Why you tell him that?

THE FRIEND. I just got out and he's fuckin' sneakin' shit up in here. Gettin' high as fuck.

KARMA. He tell you where he at?

THE FRIEND. Nope. He wouldn't. If T's still around... alive, I figure he'd find a place he'd feel protected. Understand? Play for the other team.

KARMA. ... North End Crew...

(**THE FRIEND** *nods.*)

THE FRIEND. Can I ask you somethin'?

KARMA. What?

THE FRIEND. Why you lookin' for somebody I just tole you ain't said shit about you long as I've known him?

KARMA. I got this notepad, see? I write down every nigga that's done me wrong.

THE FRIEND. Damn. How many pages – you got it that bad?

KARMA. Terrell's the only nigga whose name got crossed off the list, again and again. He fuckin' fought for me to forgive him.

THE FRIEND. What you gonna say to him when he sees you?

KARMA. I thought about this. First I'll be like, "Yo, T! What the fuck, man? You hidin' from a nigga?" Just like jokin' with him. I'd probably be happy, but won't show that shit. Then I'd be like, "What happened? Where you been?" Ya know? He'll tell me where he been. I'd tell him where I been. All the shit we missed. And hopefully, hopefully, we start feelin' like the old times. When we was tight, understand? I hope... I hope... And then, I'd probably get real serious. And then I'd just come out with it...

(*She can't get it out.*)

I'd say... I'm sorry...

THE FRIEND. Yo, you good?

KARMA. Who's choppin' onions in the mothafuckin' Chicken Shack this time a night?

THE FRIEND. I'm askin' are you good?

(*Beat.*)

KARMA. ... Yeah...

(*B. Early Christmas morning.*)

(**KARMA** *crosses the space. A* **POLICE OFFICER** *stops her.*)

POLICE. Yo!

KARMA. Officer! I was just talkin' 'bout you.

POLICE. Why you sneakin' out the back of a Chicken Shack?

KARMA. Had to relieve myself. Thanks officer. Puttin' me on blast like that.

POLICE. How old are you?

KARMA. Forty-eight. Be forty-nine tomorrow.

POLICE. You might be a minor.

KARMA. Don't ask a lady her age, officer.

POLICE. You got jokes.

KARMA. And you bored. Ain't ya?

POLICE. Why you out here this early in the morning?

KARMA. We just established this.

POLICE. What's with all them bags?

KARMA. It's Christmas, bruh. Any other questions po-lice?

POLICE. You understand why all this seems suspicious to me?

KARMA. No. I don't. Enlighten me.

POLICE. I don't like your tone.

KARMA. Don't like you assumin' shit about me.

POLICE. The situation's a little odd.

KARMA. Innocent 'til proven guilty.

POLICE. Whatever.

KARMA. Whatever? You meet your quota po-lice?

POLICE. Quota?

KARMA. Don't act confused. I know about that shit.

POLICE. I would appreciate you tellin' me what you're doin' at a Chicken Shack this time of –

KARMA. It's the end of the month, and you ain't met your quota. Am I right?

POLICE. Gimme a break, I'm pushin' overtime here.

KARMA. Where you from?

POLICE. Oh, come on kid.

KARMA. No, serious. Where you from?

(Beat.)

KARMA. No. Serious. Where you from?

(Beat. He looks out to the crowd.)

Where you from, man?

*(**KARMA** nudges him.)*

I said, "No, serious. Where you from?" And you say –

POLICE. I'm sorry. Sorry.

KARMA. *(Whispering.)* You forgot your lines again? We ran this scene like four –

POLICE. Let me... Can I...just...? You know what? Fuck it! Just gonna say it. I don't know why the playwright would write a scene like this.

(He steps from the scene.)

Sorry to stop the play, but I just got to... Because of what's about to happen next – I'm not sorry. This character I'm playing is a prop. A tool. It's shit! I played Hamlet! Vanya! I played Willy goddamn Loman! Characters of substance. With depth!

So... I'm just gonna step out here and introduce my character's backstory to all of you. And maybe none of this is true, or what the playwright intended, but it is how I crafted my character, to make him real. Fully formed. Because the writer couldn't even bother.

So... His name is Moe. He's fifty. Two kids, now adults, who hate his guts. A scraggly dog that could die any minute. A wife, who is his last and only fan. Loves golf, but got a bum hip. And he hates his job. Never been smart enough to make rank after twenty years on the force. He's seen too much. Lost two partners – friends – to gang violence. Takes his job home with him, but he never talks about it. And today is Christmas. Worst of all he wasn't supposed to work today. He's trying to remember why he became an officer. Trying his best to find that feeling again, for the past ten years. But he can't. He's tired. Grumpy. Annoyed. And then he runs into some chump given him crap because he's doin' his job. It's early fuckin' Christmas mornin', and the kid is wonderin' why she's being stopped in the street when every business on the block is closed tight. Just a simple fuckin' request!

I'm going to play him now. Like I played Willy Loman at the Irish Classical Theatre in Buffalo. Watch me, and see – and this is not to excuse what happens in this scene. I need you to understand that. That's not my point.

    (The **POLICE OFFICER** *returns to the scene.)*

Now where were we?

KARMA. Thank you.

    (They take a moment.)

Where you from?

POLICE. Not here. I'll say that.

KARMA. I got it. Don't shit where you eat.

POLICE. That's not it.

KARMA. 'Course it is. Ain't a po-lice I met been from here.

POLICE. That's not true. / That's not –

KARMA. It's cool po-lice. I get you. If there's a party, I'd trash a nigga's house worse than my own.

POLICE. What are you talkin' about?

KARMA. How does it feel walkin' The Oblong and every nigga givin' you the eye?

POLICE. Well all these po-lice are doing you a service.

KARMA. And what service you doin' but feelin' up niggas all kinda ways.

POLICE. There some bad perps in this hood.

KARMA. There some good perps too. *Sometimes* / who do bad things.

POLICE. Right, right – and *they* aren't bad?

KARMA. They *did* somethin' bad.

POLICE. And no jail. / Just let 'em go free.

KARMA. Fuck. Sure, jail a nigga, but act like he learned his fuckin' lesson, that's all I'm sayin'. / He *learned* his fuckin' lesson.

POLICE. Just *stop*! Shut your fuckin' trap! Either you tell me the deal, or I'll bust you for trespassin' on private property. You're pissin' me off.

KARMA. I wasn't tresspasin'! I'm lookin' for my brother! Alright?

POLICE. I bet.

KARMA. You bet? Here's a flyer.

(*She hands it to the* **POLICE OFFICER***. He looks it over.*)

POLICE. Terrell. How long he's been missin'?

KARMA. Over three months. He's in danger and no one's doin' shit but me. I've been all over The Oblong.

POLICE. Probably just a runaway. I suggest you get home.

KARMA. He ain't just a runaway!

POLICE. Okay, okay. Goodnight –

KARMA. I said he ain't no fuckin' runaway!

POLICE. Don't curse at me, ma'am.

KARMA. I wasn't cursin' at you.

POLICE. Don't *curse* at me!

(*Beat.*)

KARMA. Fuck you.

POLICE. What did I say?

KARMA. You said don't curse at me. And I said, "Fuck you."

POLICE. Say it again.

(*Beat. He places his hand on his gun.*)

KARMA. What you gonna do?

POLICE. Say it again.

KARMA. You ain't gonna do shit.

POLICE. Say it again.

KARMA. Ain't gonna do shit.

POLICE. Say it again. Say, "Fuck you."

> *(Beat.)*

See what happens.

> *(A long beat.* **KARMA** *really thinks about it. She really does. And then...)*

KARMA. *(Slow and deliberate.)* MERRY. CHRISTMAS.

> *(Beat.)*

POLICE. Are you crazy?

KARMA. Yup.

POLICE. Merry Christmas?

> *(He laughs.)*

KARMA. He ain't a runaway.

POLICE. Get on home. Go!

> *(She starts to go.)*

Better not see you again. I'm doin' you a favor! You know that?

> *(***KARMA*** *exits as the lights fade.)*

Exhibit D

(December 29. **MADAM PROFÍT** *throws money at the problem so that the problem is dressed in money.)*

(Amigone Funeral Home. **MADAM PROFÍT** *stands at a podium, and* **THE PROTÉGÉ**, *a young girl, seventeen, dressed beautifully, sits in a chair beside her.* **THE PROTÉGÉ** *holds an extravagant bouquet of flowers.)*

PROFÍT. What a turn out, what a turn out. I thank you all for coming. You promise food and you can fill a stadium. My pillars of the community. Entrepreneurs. Social activists, members of the city council, and concerned citizens. I am blessed to see the local news, TV and print, in attendance. Thank you. My name is Madam Rose Profít. Profít! The "o" is an "o" not an "ah" and the "t" is silent. Pro-fee.

Before we start, I'd like to take this moment to point out a special, special individual who has helped us make this afternoon possible on so little notice. Ladies and gentlemen this person humbly wished to be here with little fanfare, but I cannot resist. Without further ado, the Mayor, ladies and gentlemen. The Mayor of our wonderful metropolis.

(She points to an individual in the audience, be they a he or a she, and applauds them. She makes sure the audience does as well.)

I hope you don't mind me saying this, Mayor. But we had a private meeting recently, and we hit it off, like we've known each other for years. And when the Mayor heard my idea and poured over my proposal, this generous human being pledged money, courted the city council, and this event was born! I am moved to tears by the trust and generosity of this wonderful human being.

(She tries for tears. It doesn't happen.)

PROFÍT. Moved to tears. I cannot match this amazing gift at the moment, but...

> *(She signals her **PROTÉGÉ**, who brings over the bouquet of flowers to the Mayor.)*

Now stand! Stand up and be recognized. Thank you. Thank you. I cannot wait to share with you the work I'm doing. It will be worth every penny. Thank you. You can sit.

What the Mayor has so smartly recognized is my school for the troubled children of The Oblong. Madam Profít's School for the Derelict will take the lost and forgotten children of this city and mold them into contributing members of society. But this school is only an idea, members of the city council. It needs capitol to be realized. Charity. Subsidies. Grants.

So today, I will present to you, one of my progeny. She who will serve as an example of what this school can be. This fine young woman to my right is Chanel. I found her shivering in the cold. Exhausted by the streets. Used up by men and drugs, and blind to any sort of hope. Her son, bound to a wheelchair by gang violence, she neglected. Her life in shambles.

But I would not let her go astray. I saw in her great potential. So I took her in. I fed her, cleaned her up, detoxed her of the horrible heroin, and steered her back towards education, and building a positive relationship with her son. She is enrolled in college by my wallet, an apartment of her own by my wallet, and works as receptionist to Amigone Funeral Home, Inc. What was once just another statistic...she has found her autonomy, wears that electric smile, and impeccable fashion. A round of applause if you will for the new Chanel! Go on, stand up child. Stand up, it's for you! All for you!

> *(She doesn't stand.* **PROFÍT** *whispers to her.)*
What's the matter with you? Stand up!

THE PROTÉGÉ. I can't –

PROFÍT. Go on, you silly girl.

THE PROTÉGÉ. I'm nervous –

PROFÍT. She's nervous! Bless her. Applause. Applause, please. Clap her to her feet. Go on! Now let's support the dear child as she speaks a few words of where she was and where she's heading, thanks to me and Madam Profit's School for the Derelict. Go on child, stand up.

> *(She does not.)*

Chanel! This is emotional for her.

THE PROTÉGÉ. I...can't...

PROFÍT. Of course you can, I wrote out – *WE* wrote out your speech together.

THE PROTÉGÉ. Madam Pro-fee –

PROFÍT. There are note cards on the podium. Don't embarrass me.

> *(She yanks her up to the podium.)*

Ladies and gentlemen. Chanel.

> **(MADAM PROFÍT** *sits.* **THE PROTÉGÉ** *just stands there, looking out into the crowd. It's an uncomfortable silence.)*

Talk! Read the damn cards.

THE PROTÉGÉ. Hi. I'm...

> **(MADAM PROFÍT** *stands. Holds the flash cards out to her.* **THE PROTÉGÉ** *looks at the cards. Looks to* **MADAM PROFÍT.** *It seems as if she'll say something. It lingers.* **THE PROTÉGÉ** *vomits all over* **MADAM PROFÍT**'s *dress.)*

PROFÍT. Oh my God. Oh my God. / Oh my God.

THE PROTÉGÉ. I'm sorry. So sorry. I was nervous –

PROFÍT. Don't just stand there. Get me something you waste!

> **(MADAM PROFÍT** *uses a handkerchief.)*

THE PROTÉGÉ. Excuse me.

PROFÍT. I told you to get me something.

THE PROTÉGÉ. "You waste." That's what you said to me.

PROFÍT. I've got better insults than that, my dear. How dare you! In front of all of these people! The Mayor! I should have left you and your retarded kid on the goddamn corner! Stupid girl. Do you realize what you've done?

> *(**THE PROTÉGÉ** absorbs this.)*

I told you to get me something.

> *(**THE PROTÉGÉ** approaches the podium.)*

THE PROTÉGÉ. Ladies and Gentlemen...

PROFÍT. What are you doing?

THE PROTÉGÉ. As she said, my name is Chanel. And I am thankful to Mrs. Profit –

PROFÍT. Madam Pro-fee, child. The "o" is an "o" not an "ah" –

THE PROTÉGÉ. So thankful!

PROFÍT. Go on.

THE PROTÉGÉ. Thankful, for the two hundred dollars she slipped in my hand when she met me.

PROFÍT. ... What...

THE PROTÉGÉ. I just met this bitch on Tuesday!

PROFÍT. Watch it.

THE PROTÉGÉ. She lyin' – you lyin'...

PROFÍT. That's / that's not true, ladies and gentleman.

THE PROTÉGÉ. Where the Mayor at?

PROFÍT. Stop it!

THE PROTÉGÉ. She played you bro –

PROFÍT. I shoulda left you on the corner!

> *(**THE PROTÉGÉ** approaches the Mayor. **PROFÍT** follows.)*

THE PROTÉGÉ. She told me Mayor –

PROFÍT. I didn't! / Did not –

THE PROTÉGÉ. She promised me *bank*, / ya heard? Bank!

PROFÍT. That's a bald face lie!

THE PROTÉGÉ. All I gotta do –

PROFÍT. Shut up. Quiet! / She's lying! *She's* the liar!

THE PROTÉGÉ. "All I got to do is pretend!" she said.

>   (**MADAM PROFÍT** *pulls at* **THE PROTÉGÉ**.)

PROFÍT. You're gone, / young lady!

THE PROTÉGÉ. Pretend! / That's what she said!

PROFÍT. Out! I never wanna see you again!

>   (**MADAM PROFÍT** *tries to shove her off, but she's
>   not much stronger.* **THE PROTÉGÉ** *yanks her
>   hand back.*)

THE PROTÉGÉ. I think I've said enough.

>   (**THE PROTÉGÉ** *exits.* **MADAM PROFÍT** *spies the
>   audience and crosses over to the podium.
>   Looks out.*)

PROFÍT. If you think I am done...*finished...* I am not. I am
never –

>   (*Blackout.*)

Scene Six

(*December 31.* **KARMA** *infiltrates the North End Crew finding herself that much closer to her missing foster brother.*)

(*On the corner. The marketplace is open.*)

(**KARMA** *hangs with two young men; one older than she,* **DEATH**, *twenties, wears a cap the reads "death" in big block letters; the other,* **YOUTH**, *probably fourteen, is much younger than she, nervous, and very green. All check their shoulders.*)

DEATH. … She was all like, "You. Assholes." Says shit like, "I find police."

YOUTH. Word?

KARMA. She was sayin' shit in French or some…what was it?

DEATH. German.

KARMA. Nice, German.

YOUTH. You stupid. Can't tell the difference between German and French?

KARMA. Shut the fuck up! This was a long ass time ago.

YOUTH. What happened?

DEATH. So I'm like still blockin' the graffiti and shit, and this tourist ain't scared of nothin'!

KARMA. Lady was gangsta!

DEATH. She was fienin' for that graffiti artist. Ain't even the good shit.

KARMA. Nigga from a different country.

YOUTH. And what country's that?

KARMA. Why you diggin' at me?

DEATH. Can we stay on topic?

KARMA. So he was like you pay, or you go.

DEATH. Meanwhile, Ms. Swastika got all kinda pictures of our hands, fuckin' legs, my dope ass kicks.

YOUTH. Shoulda charged her for *that*!

DEATH. This bitch fuckin' had the balls to say, "How dare you!" Said, "This man did this for you people."

YOUTH. "You people." Oh, shit...

KARMA. And?

DEATH. So I was like, what you mean, "You people"? And she was like, "Black people."

YOUTH. Oh shit!

KARMA. This nigga got all proper then. He was like, "I don't like that phrase. You people."

DEATH. And she was ramblin' 'bout how she's seen all us in movies and TV, shootin' and killin' each other.

KARMA. And this lady's like, "I feel bad for you."

YOUTH. Wow.

DEATH. Bad for us. I fuckin' lost it!

KARMA. This nigga was just yellin', yellin', yellin'. And I don't know what happened, but this bitch's high powered camera was in pieces on the ground.

DEATH. I knocked that piece of shit right out of her hands. And then we both was yellin'.

KARMA. That was messed man. You took that too far.

YOUTH. Shit seems the right distance to me.

DEATH. Thank you!

KARMA. We ain't even at the end of this. This nigga right here –

DEATH. You know what? "Fuck it!" I said. "Give me your damn fannie pack."

YOUTH. She had a fannie pack?! Yo!

KARMA. He snatched it right off her waist! *That* shit was funny.

YOUTH. Holy shit! What she do?

KARMA. Well she tried to snatch it back, but nigga right here was the Heisman, understand? She went left, he went right. She was down, my nigga was *flyin'*.

DEATH. Poof! Out! We had that cartoon dust behind us, we was so fast.

YOUTH. Cartoon dust! Yo, you got some balls.

KARMA. That's so fucked, though.

YOUTH. Welcome to America!

DEATH. Ha! You a fool!

KARMA. Bet she wasn't as fast as Terrell, though.

> (**DEATH** *stops laughing. He doesn't find this funny.*)

DEATH. ... Terrell...

> (*It grows quiet. And then...*)

Four or five years, K-Nice. And suddenly you hittin' me up. Outta nowhere and shit.

KARMA. Needed the hook-up. 'Sides I miss hangin'. You a big dude now.

DEATH. Mmhmm.

KARMA. You know me...

> (*Beat.*)

DEATH. We packin' up soon. I gotta get my New Year's on.

KARMA. You got plans?

DEATH. Just me and my moms. Hangin' at the house. You?

> (*BOOM! Gunfire? The* **YOUTH** *jumps.*)

You cool, man?

YOUTH. I'm cool... You know...

DEATH. You think you up for this?

> (**KARMA** *laughs.*)

KARMA. Don't look it.

YOUTH. Don't laugh bitch! / I'm 'bout it I said.

DEATH. Alright, let's get to it. Imma come with the honesty real quick like. This is a business, my niggas. And that may not sound like a fresh idea to you, but most niggas don't understand that. They don't take this shit seriously. You get up, you show up, you do your shit. And you keep it consistent like, you know what I'm sayin'? You two are employees and I'm your on-site supervisor, right?

YOUTH & KARMA. Yeah.

DEATH. And all these niggas out here got different skills and talents beneficial to the product we pushin', and the customers we serve. Me, I'm over ya'll, and there's somebody over me. And that travels up a chain all the way to the CEO.

> *(Boom! The* **YOUTH** *jumps again.)*

It's cool, man. Just fireworks.

YOUTH. I know. Fuck.

KARMA. You almost backflipped!

YOUTH. Shut the fuck up!

KARMA. Okay. Kid's on edge.

> *(Boom! Another. The* **YOUTH** *fidgets.* **KARMA** *laughs.)*

DEATH. Calm down. Damn. Now where was I?

YOUTH. The CEO.

DEATH. My nigga. Somebody you'll never know. And why's that?

YOUTH. Things changed after they locked up all the OGs.

KARMA. Word. Everything got fucked! Loyalty, leadership.

DEATH. The rules done changed. You niggas know them?

YOUTH. Yup.

DEATH. How you know? I ain't told you.

YOUTH. I been in this for a minute.

DEATH. Oh. You have, little man?

YOUTH. Hell yeah.

DEATH. Then you should know there ain't no fuckin' rules to the game. *None.* Understand?

YOUTH. Yeah.

DEATH. And that shit means no stability.

YOUTH. Yeah.

DEATH. And also you gotta define what a win is to you. Understand me. 'Cause the majority of all this is losin'.

(Boom! Another.)

'Cause there's other roads you could choose. You understand me?

(Boom!)

KARMA. I got you.

DEATH. Young buck?

YOUTH. ... Yeah...

DEATH. This business is balance. It's important to be inconspicuous, but it's also important to be known.

KARMA. Just like Terrell. Am I right? He's fuckin' known.

YOUTH. What's his story?

KARMA. From what I heard –

DEATH. Can we focus? Damn. Gotta be known, lil' man. You gotta build street cred. Understand?

YOUTH. How I do that?

DEATH. Don't be a sucka!

KARMA. Word.

DEATH. Straight up. Don't be a sucka. There's niggas out here that'll clown you. They will try all sorts of shit.

YOUTH. I got you.

DEATH. And to avoid that shit is cred. And to get that you got to earn it. And to earn it, you got to put in work.

KARMA. Get up, get to work, do your shit.

DEATH. More than that. I'm talkin' 'bout fear. Fear, K-Nice.

(Beat.)

That shit makes you known my nigga.

KARMA. That's truth, though. You known on the block. Got niggas tremblin'.

DEATH. I ain't as crazy as that nigga Petey, though.

KARMA. Oh shit Petey! I ain't heard about that nigga for a minute.

YOUTH. Petey?

KARMA. Petey's buckwild!

DEATH. That nigga used to say his granddad used to fuck his dad growin' up. So then, Petey's dad beat the shit out of Petey.

KARMA. Shit's a cycle.

> *(Boom!)*

YOUTH. The fuck man! It's not even midnight yet! What they doin'?!

> *(KARMA laughs.)*

KARMA. What's your problem?

YOUTH. Nothin'!

KARMA. It's just fuckin' firecrackers. Nigga got that soldier shit.

YOUTH. I'm good. Damn.

DEATH. You a soldier, young buck?

YOUTH. At war for my life.

DEATH. All us are. Best believe.

YOUTH. My cousin's been to war. He got back home and we was chillin', right? Goin' to the shop for a drink. And we walkin', we hear like this gunshot or somethin'. A car backfired. That's what it was. But my cousin and I were straight on the ground, fuckin' flat and shakin'. We were buggin'. And then we straight lost it. Laughin'! And he ask me "You been to war, too?" And I tole him, "I been in The Oblong all my life." And he said to me, "Ain't no fuckin' difference."

DEATH. Well, keep that shit to yourself.

YOUTH. I got you.

KARMA. Tell him 'bout T.

DEATH. Yo, what the fuck, K-Nice?!

KARMA. What?

DEATH. "What?" Why you droppin' Terrell's name like that? He been gone a week.

KARMA. That long?

DEATH. Yeah. Over that. What?

KARMA. I just think it's relevant to what we talkin' 'bout right now.

DEATH. You even know what the fuck he did?

KARMA. No. But some of them niggas earlier kept mentionin' Terrell, and –

DEATH. Who? What niggas mention Terrell?

KARMA. Ah, come on man. You know who –

DEATH. Who?

KARMA. What's up with you?

DEATH. What's up with me? You suddenly appear outta fuckin' nowhere and keep mentionin' Terrell every fuckin' sentence, when I don't wanna hear his name.

KARMA. I got you.

DEATH. Nah, nah. Nah you don't...

KARMA. What, man?

DEATH. You right. Terrell fucked up. Fucked up real bad. Came up on us actin' all hot shit, like he the best thing since Hip Hop. Bragged he jumped some nigga in his lady's own crib. Laughin' 'bout gettin' that nigga arrested. Said he tired of doin' it alone. Wanted to G-up. So we let him in, and I was the one to show him 'round. Once we got on the streets, that nigga was clumsy. He was nervous. A fuckin' baby.

KARMA. Yeah. That's what I heard. Terrell couldn't –

DEATH. You fuckin' know this nigga or some shit? That it?

KARMA. Naw man, naw. Just curious –

DEATH. Since you so curious about your boy Terrell, K-Nice, let me enlighten you, so maybe you'll keep your mouth shut.

KARMA. Look, I was just –

DEATH. Fuck that. "You was just." That nigga pussied out. We was slingin' shit on the corner, just like we doin' now, and T was runner. Well outta nowhere these niggas swoop in and start poundin' us, straight tryin' to jack us of our shit. We ain't even seen the dudes comin', and we fuckin' tryin' to catch up with what's goin' on, and I spot your boy T standin' frozen 'cross the street. Just watchin' these dudes take us. I mean just clown us unconscious. And I'm yellin' at him, "Yo! Yo! Get in this T! Get in this!" And next thing I see? That nigga's a ghost. Straight vanished!

KARMA. Daaamn. Sorry I brought him –

DEATH. If I find him – *when* I find him. He's done. I'm talkin' Biblical shit. I'm takin' his eye.

KARMA. … I…

DEATH. You be runnin' your mouth a bit too much, my nigga. I remember that about you.

KARMA. I'll stop talkin' 'bout –

DEATH. Nah. Shut the fuck up.

KARMA. But I –

DEATH. Just keep runnin' that mouth.

KARMA. Look, man –

DEATH. And I wanna know what *you* gonna do about it, lil' man?

(**DEATH** *looks to the* **YOUTH.**)

YOUTH. Me.

DEATH. Yeah. You.

KARMA. I apologized man –

DEATH. What's your street cred gonna be lil' man?

KARMA. You funny.

(**DEATH** *pushes the* **YOUTH** *towards* **KARMA.**)

DEATH. I said she runnin' her mouth a bit too fuckin' much, lil' man.

KARMA. Stop playin'.

DEATH. What's your rep gonna be? Go 'head. I got your back. I'll tell *all* the niggas 'bout you.

KARMA. Look, I'm sorry, fuck. It's New Year's. Let's just chill.

DEATH. Don't disappoint me, nigga. Like Terrell.

>　(*The* **YOUTH** *gets in* **KARMA***'s face.*)

Now we talkin'. Oh shit!

KARMA. Oh it's like that, young buck. Okay.

DEATH. Let's do this! Let's go!

KARMA. You don't wanna fuck with me nigga. I ain't afraid to fight. And I fight dirty. Only stupid niggas believe in a fair fight. I like a little hurt-sport.

>　(*The* **YOUTH** *pushes her. They're on the floor. They wrestle at matched strengths. A crowd gathers. They feed the fury. It seems like minutes but it is only seconds...*)
>
>　(*Blam!!!*)
>
>　(*A firework? The crowd disperses. The* **YOUTH** *quickly stands, gun in hand.* **DEATH** *signals* **YOUTH** *to run. They do.*)
>
>　(**KARMA** *does not move. She just lies there. Sirens blare in the distance.*)
>
>　(*Fireworks go off.*)
>
>　(*Or gunshots.*)
>
>　(*Fireworks go off.*)
>
>　(*Or gunshots.*)
>
>　(*Time passes.*)
>
>　(*There is no curtain lowered.*)
>
>　(*There is no blackout.*)
>
>　(*There is no curtain call.*)

(There's just possible fireworks.)

(And **KARMA.***)*

(Dead...)

End of Play